This Fantastical Colouring Book belongs to:

_____

Fantastical Colouring

Colouring Book for Adults

Volume One

Designed and illustrated by Imran Mughal

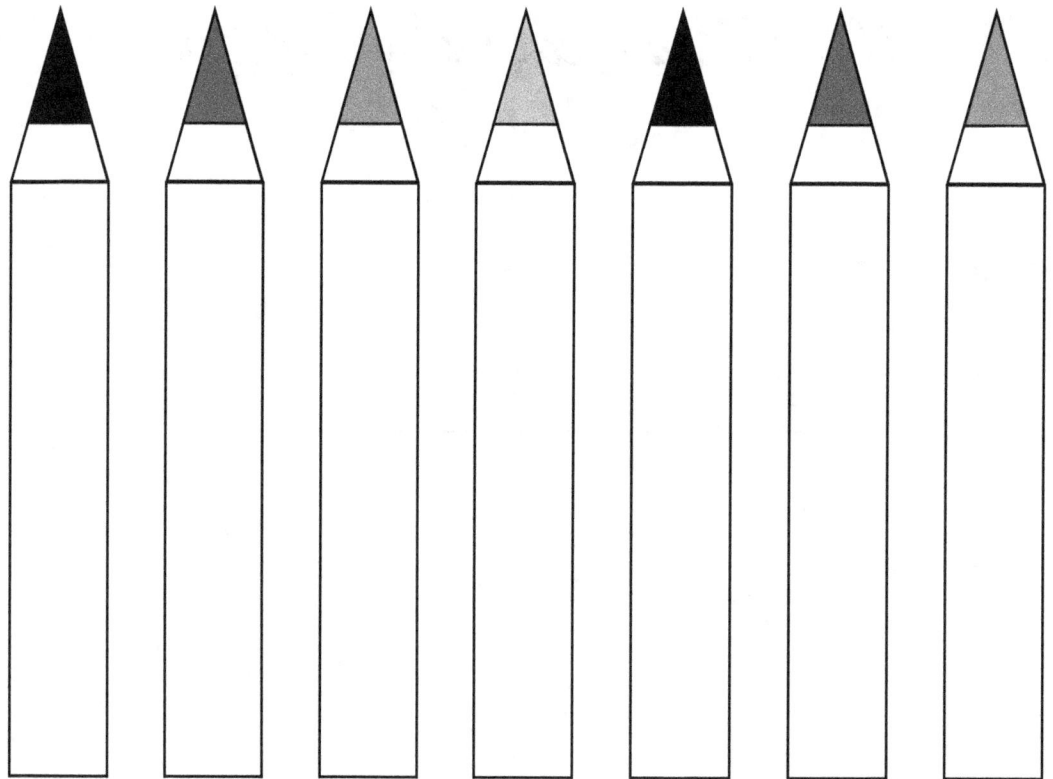

Copyright © 2020 Imran Mughal. All rights reserved. No part of this publication may be reproduced, distributed, or transmitted, in any form or by any means, including photocopying, recording, or other electronic or mechanical methods.

Coloured Pencils

My recommended colouring medium to use for this colouring book is *artists' quality coloured pencils* either wax based or oil based and applying dry blending techniques. The back page of each illustration is left blank to avoid scratching through and minimise smudging of colours.

Scan the QR codes below to easily find my recommended brands of coloured pencils. If you cannot get the recommended pencils, then try to find alternative artists' quality pencils - avoid cheap pencils as these will not produce good results.

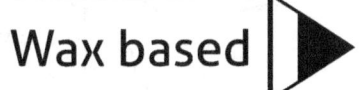  

To achieve the best results from the above coloured pencils, you can watch my *Coloured Pencils For Beginners Course* and learn the techniques to blend, layer and use colour theory to produce beautiful vibrant values that you can apply in this colouring book! You can watch the classes on coloured pencils exclusively for FREE via the following QR codes:

Wet mediums are NOT RECOMMENDED for this colouring book such as alcohol markers, felt tips, pens, inks, watercolour, gouache, acrylic paint, oil paint etc. If you really want to use such mediums, then try them out on the blank pages at the end of the book to test their suitability before starting to colour in the pages to avoid disappointment!

Colour Swatch

Always a good idea to test out your colours before you begin colouring in!
Test your colours here and write down the colour names:

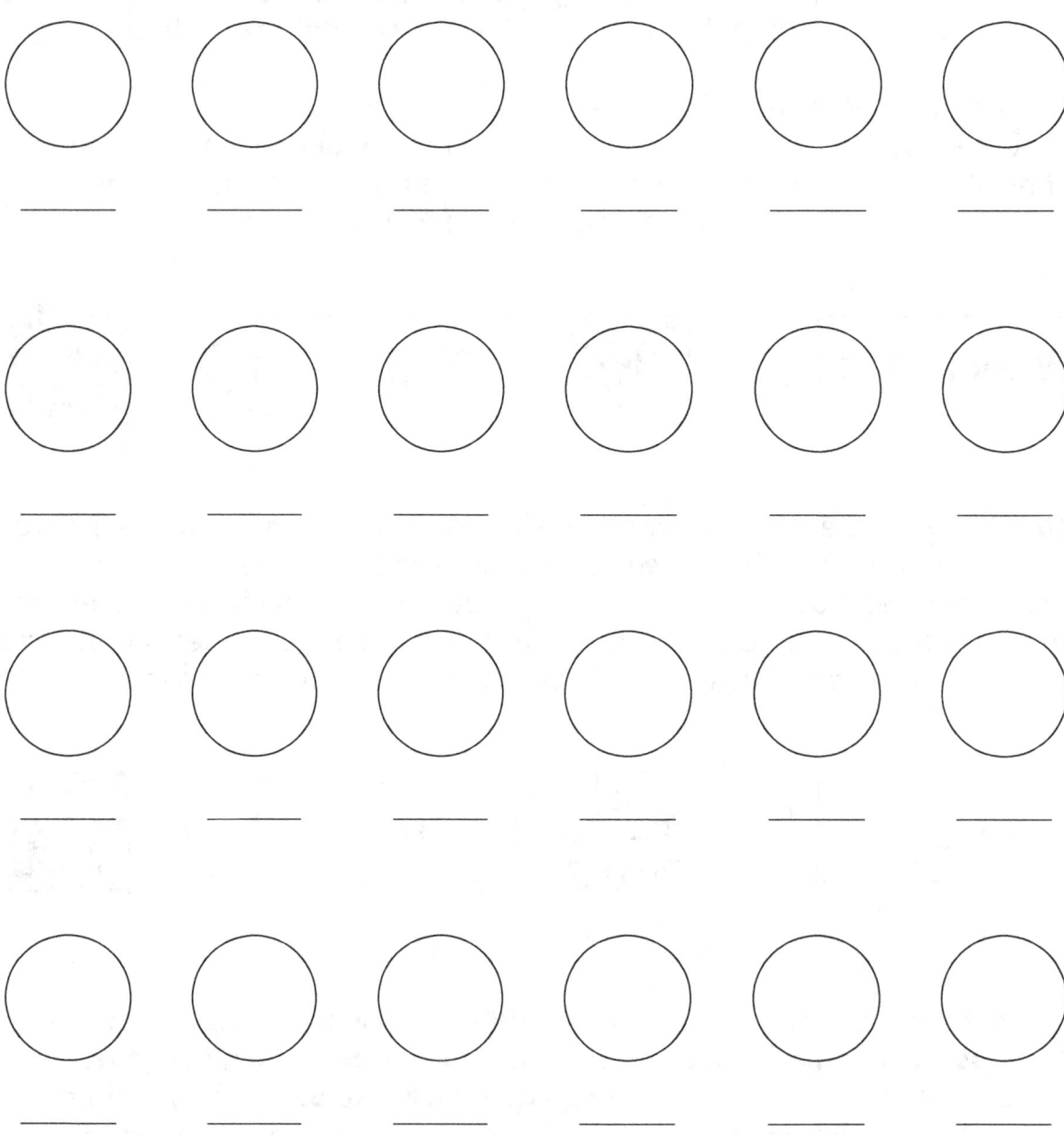

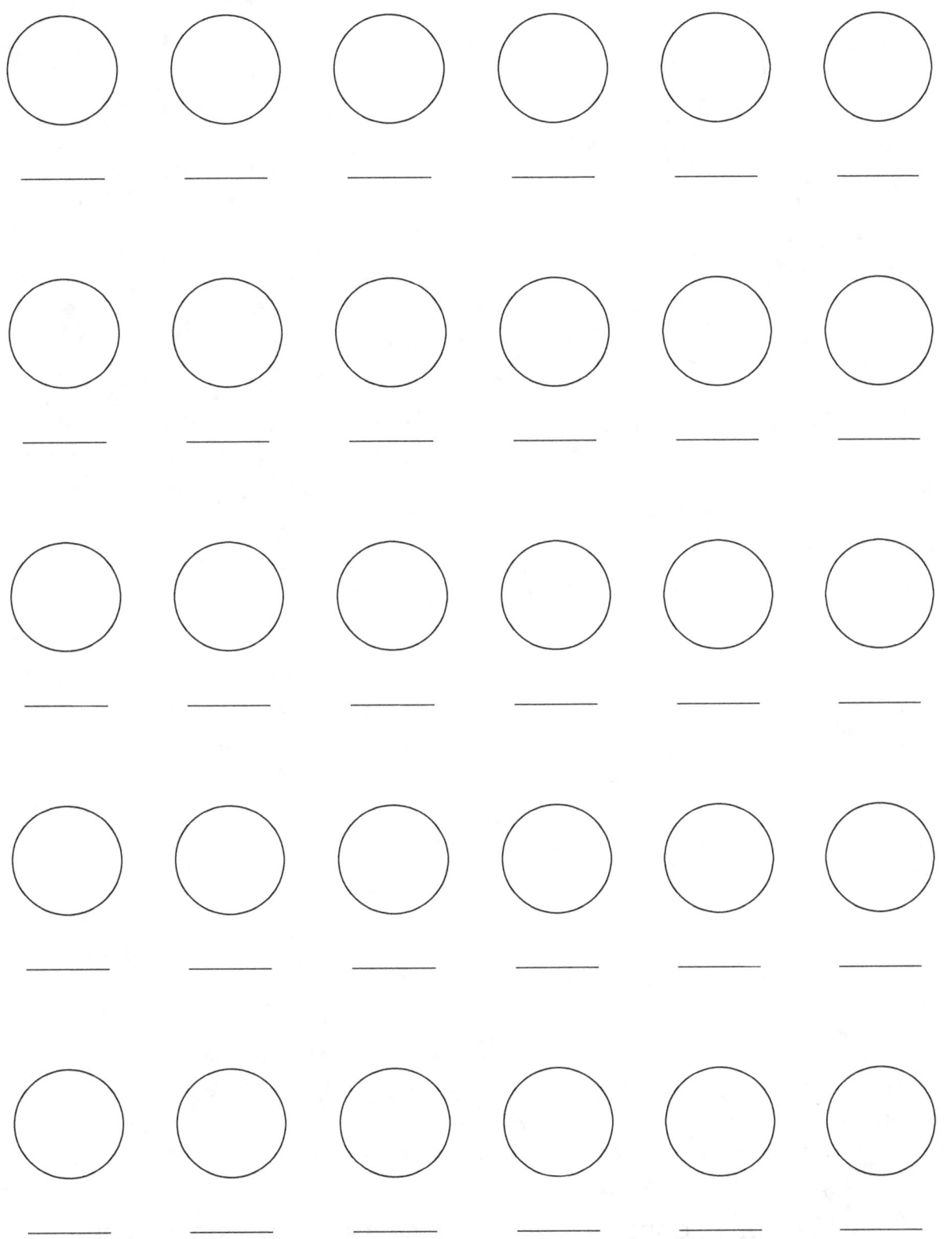

Let the colouring begin...

01

When you're done, take a pic and share on Instagram using
#FantasticalColouring

Copyright©2020 Imran Mughal

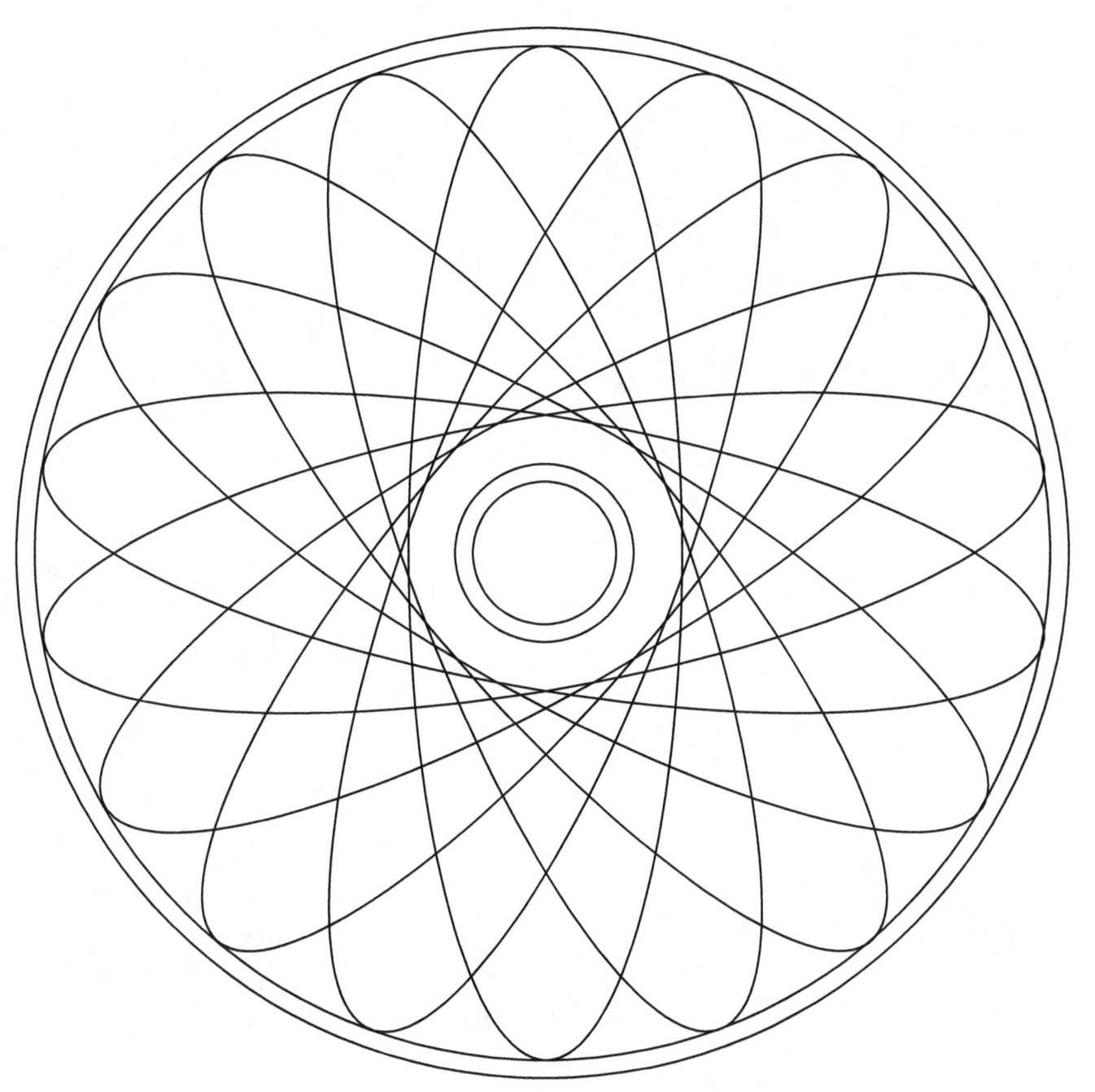

02

When you're done, take a pic and share on Instagram using
#FantasticalColouring

Copyright©2020 Imran Mughal

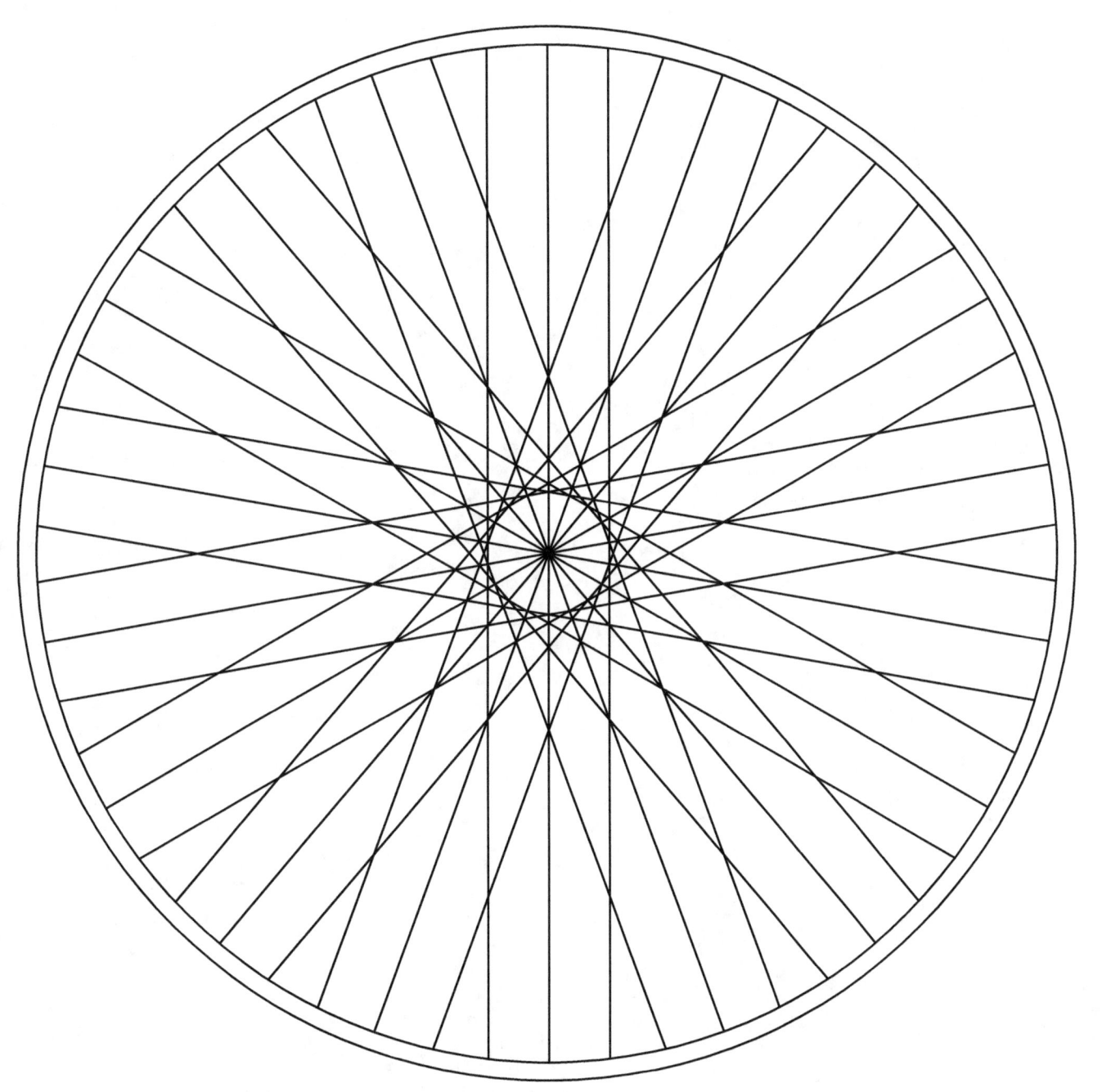

03

When you're done, take a pic and share on Instagram using
#FantasticalColouring

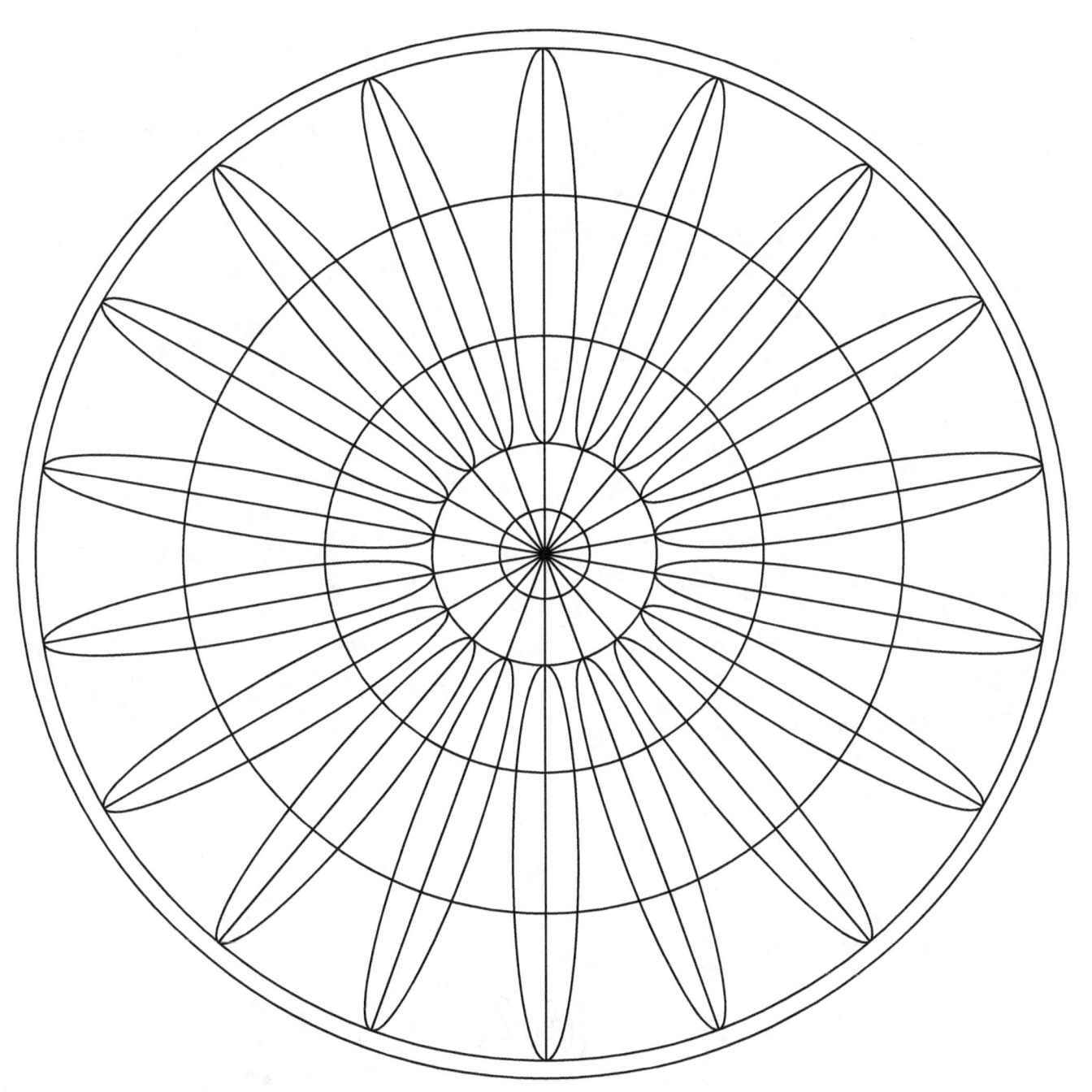

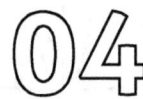

When you're done, take a pic and share on Instagram using
#FantasticalColouring

Copyright©2020 Imran Mughal

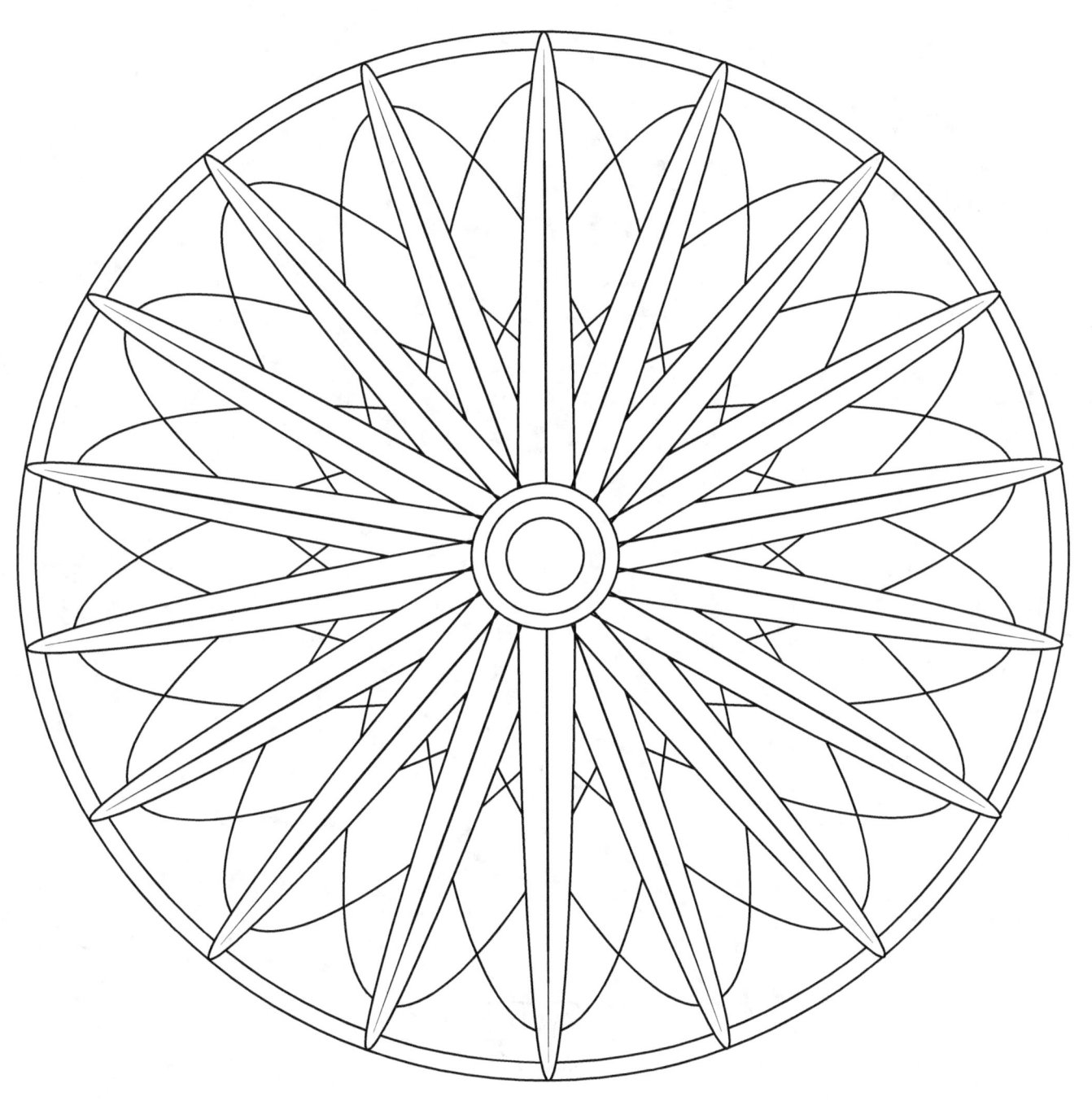

05

When you're done, take a pic and share on Instagram using
#FantasticalColouring

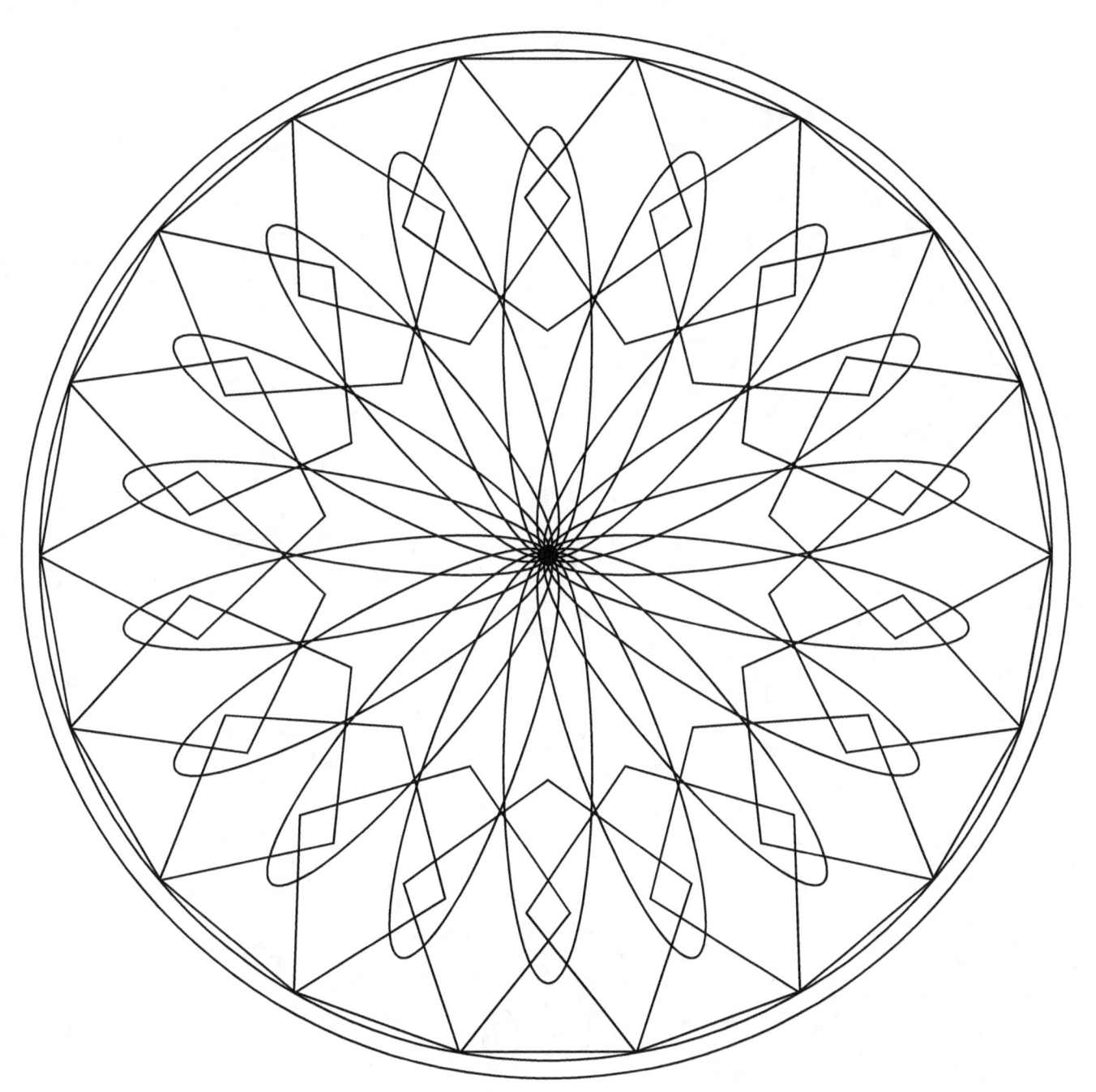

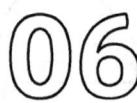

When you're done, take a pic and share on Instagram using
#FantasticalColouring

Copyright©2020 Imran Mughal

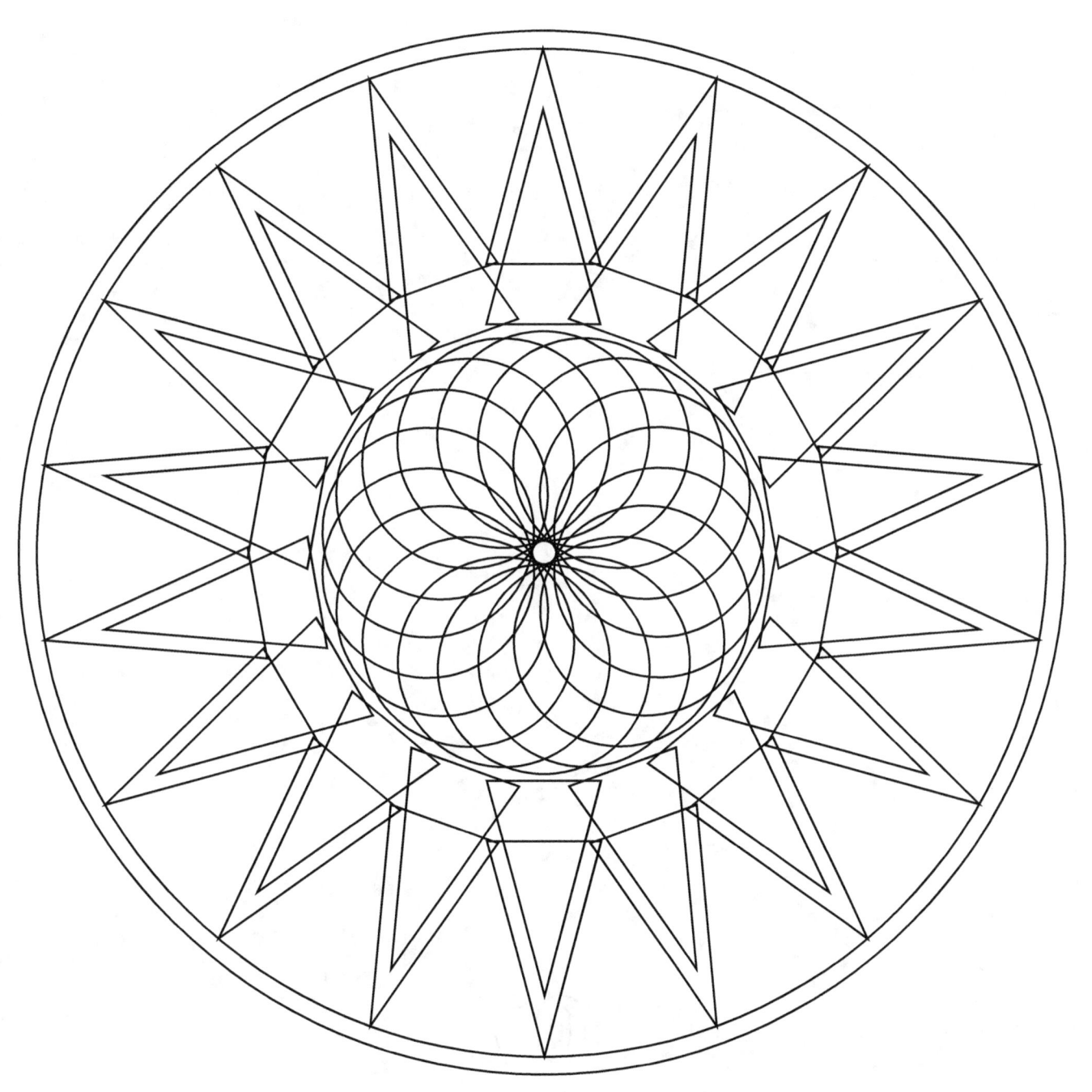

07

When you're done, take a pic and share on Instagram using
#FantasticalColouring

Copyright©2020 Imran Mughal

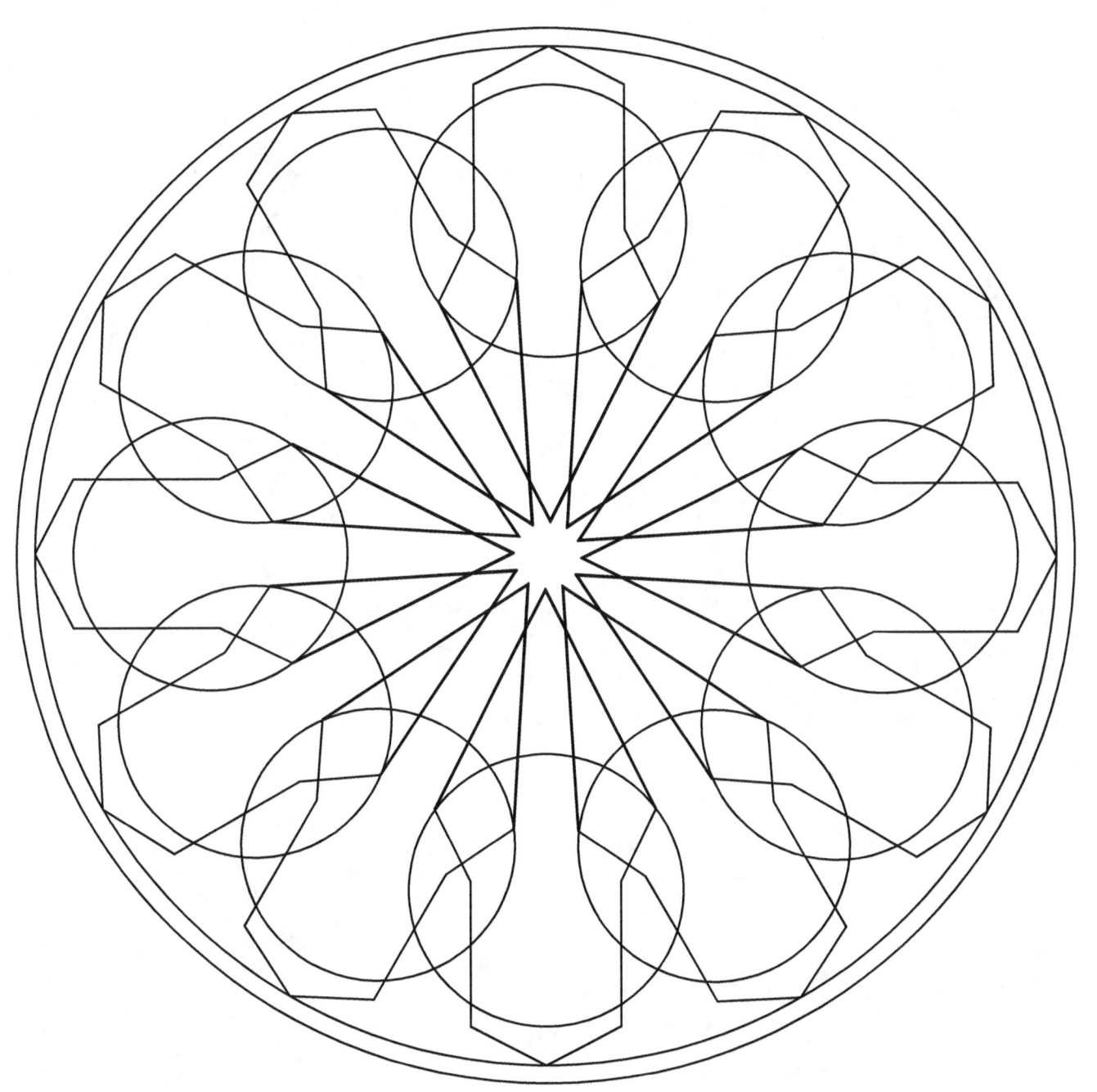

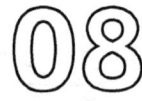

When you're done, take a pic and share on Instagram using
#FantasticalColouring

Copyright©2020 Imran Mughal

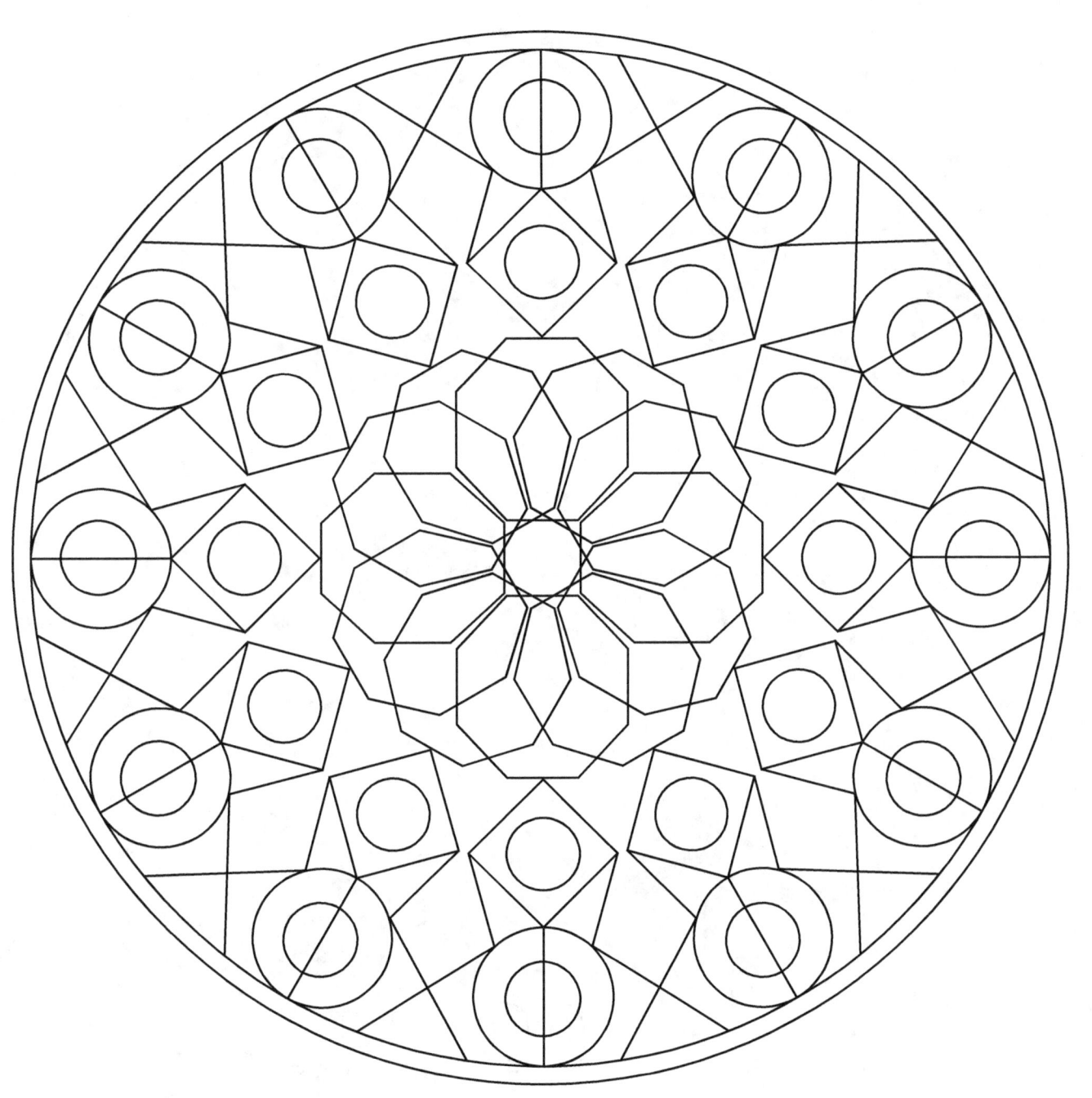

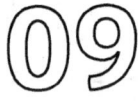

When you're done, take a pic and share on Instagram using
#FantasticalColouring

Copyright©2020 Imran Mughal

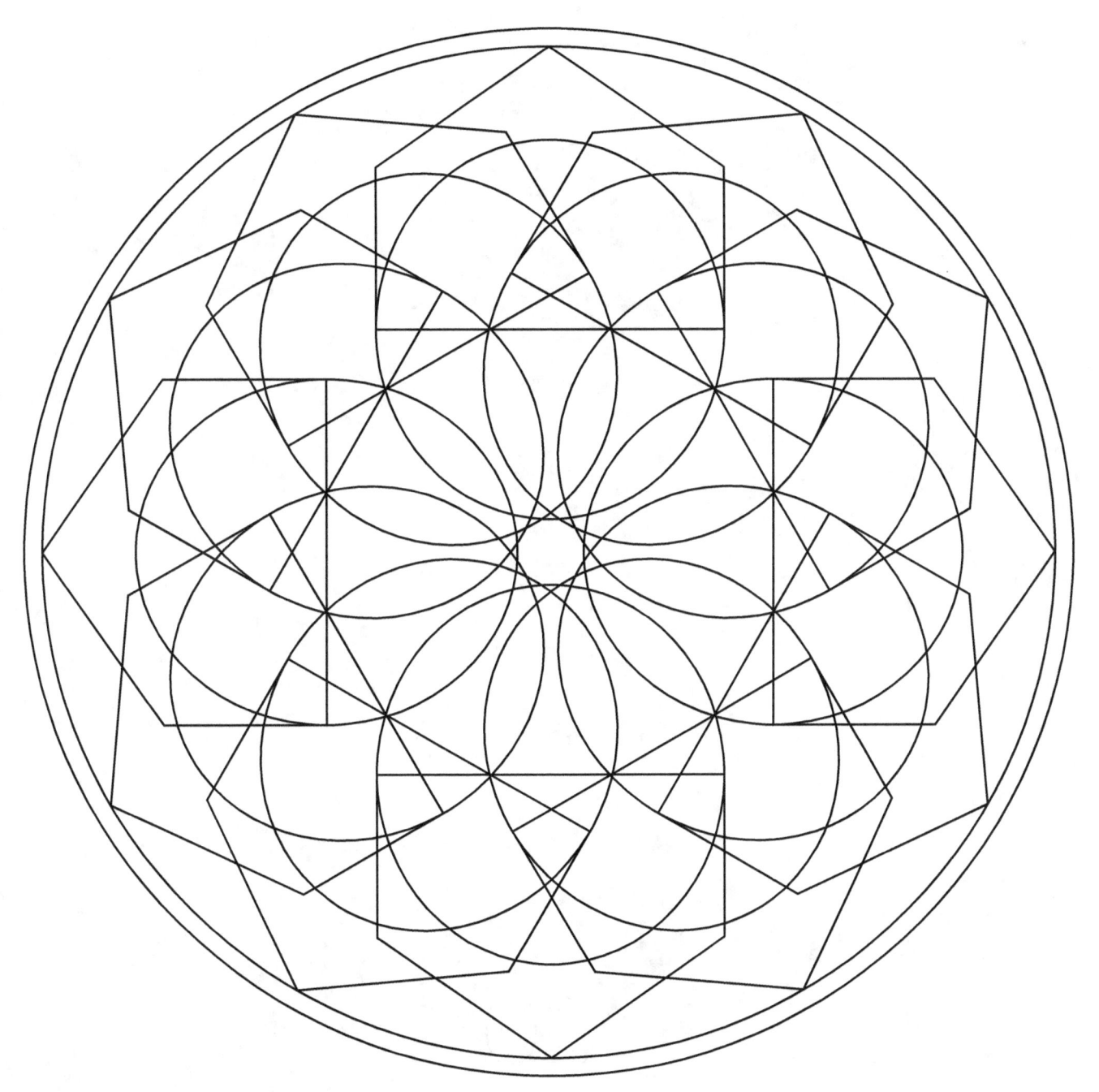

10

When you're done, take a pic and share on Instagram using
#FantasticalColouring

Copyright©2020 Imran Mughal

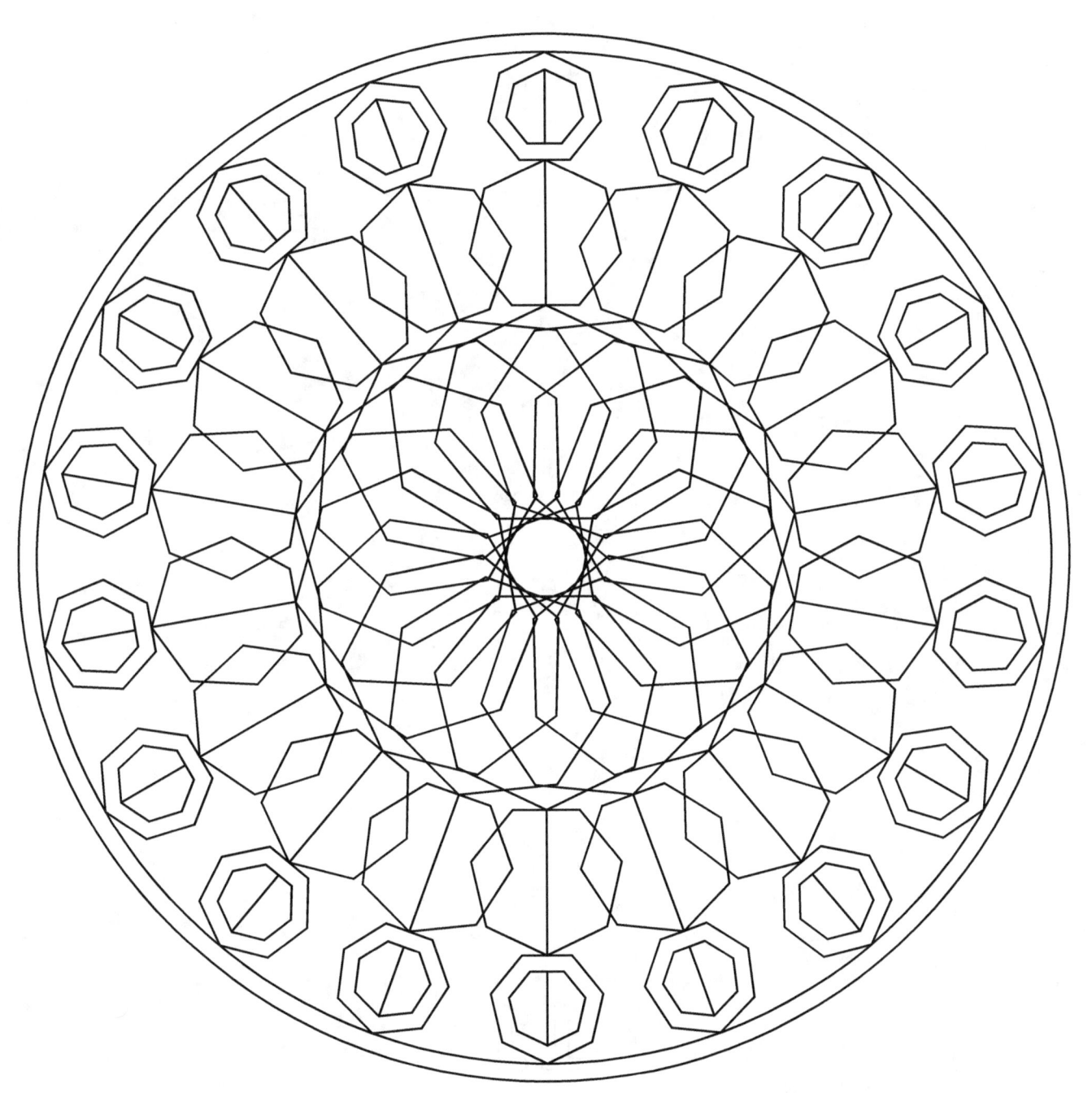

11

When you're done, take a pic and share on Instagram using
#FantasticalColouring

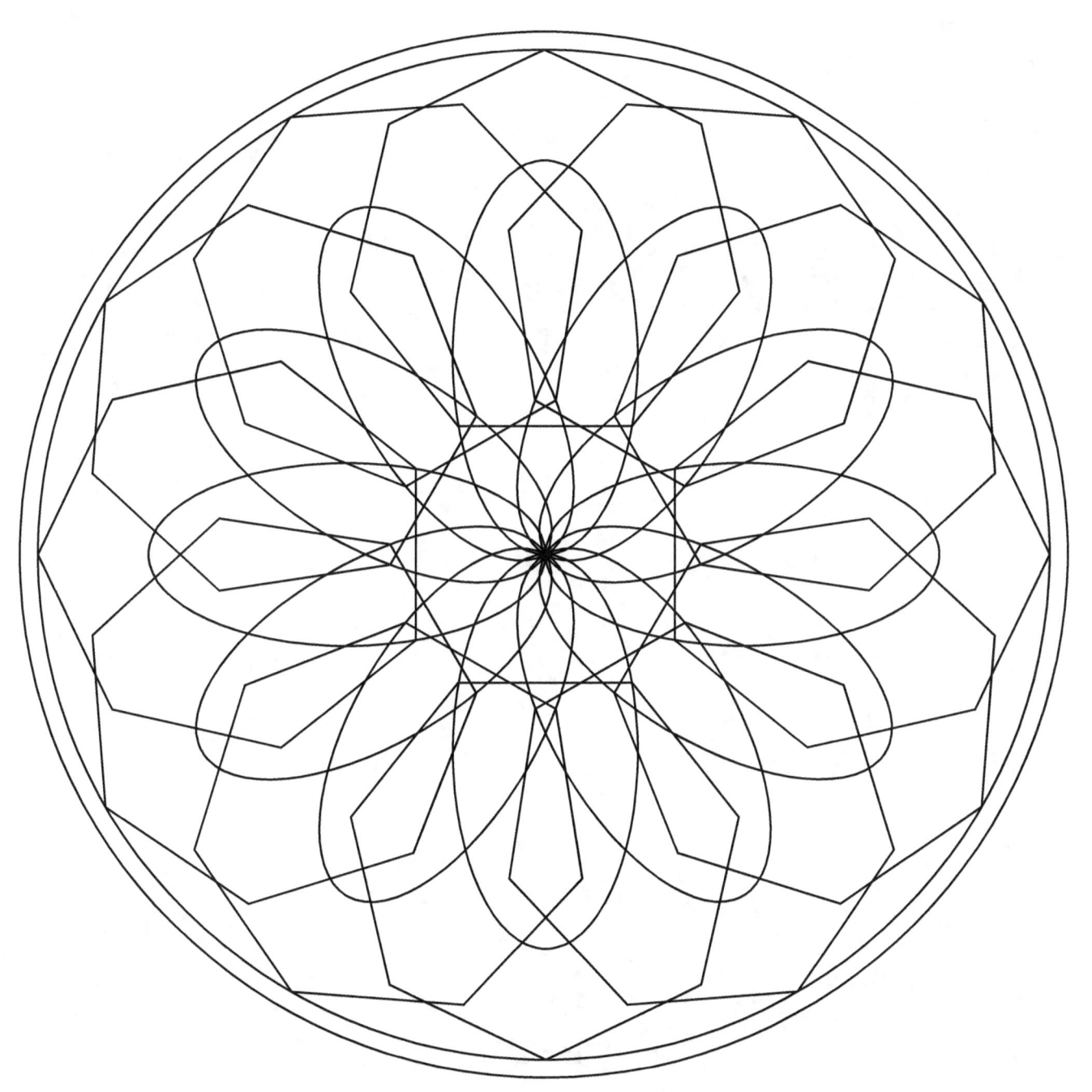

12

When you're done, take a pic and share on Instagram using
#FantasticalColouring

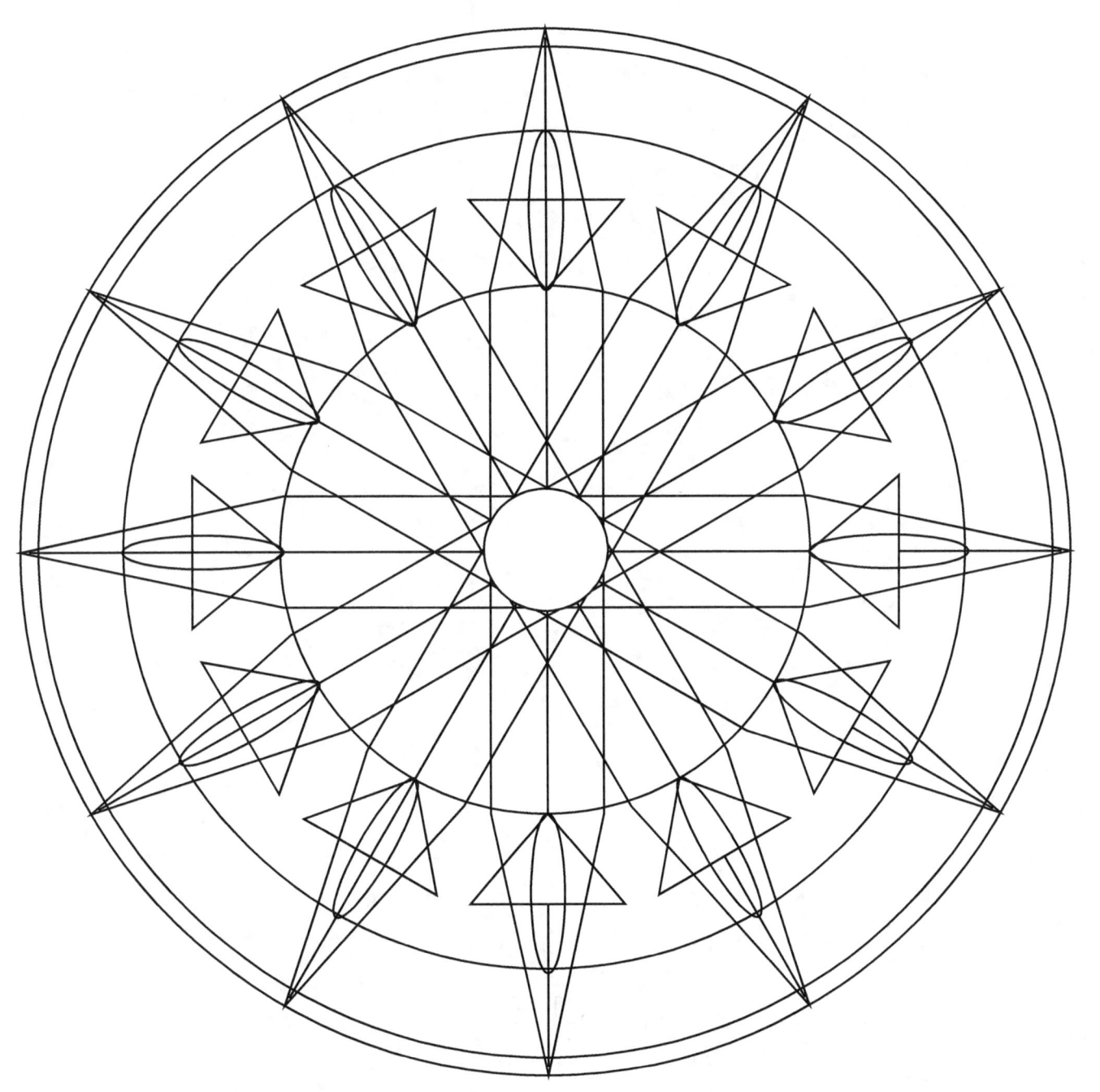

When you're done, take a pic and share on Instagram using
#FantasticalColouring

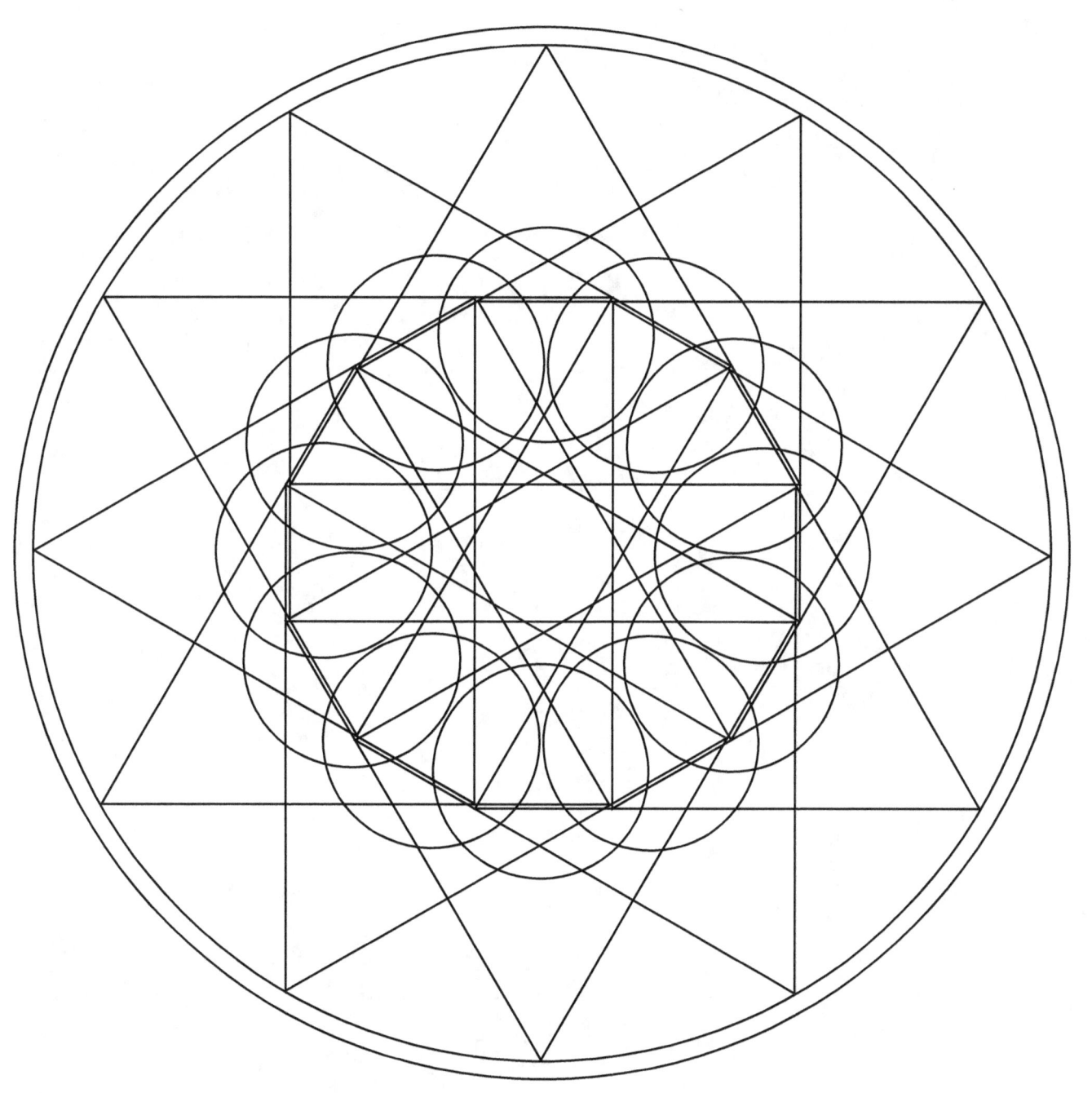

14

When you're done, take a pic and share on Instagram using
#FantasticalColouring

Copyright©2020 Imran Mughal

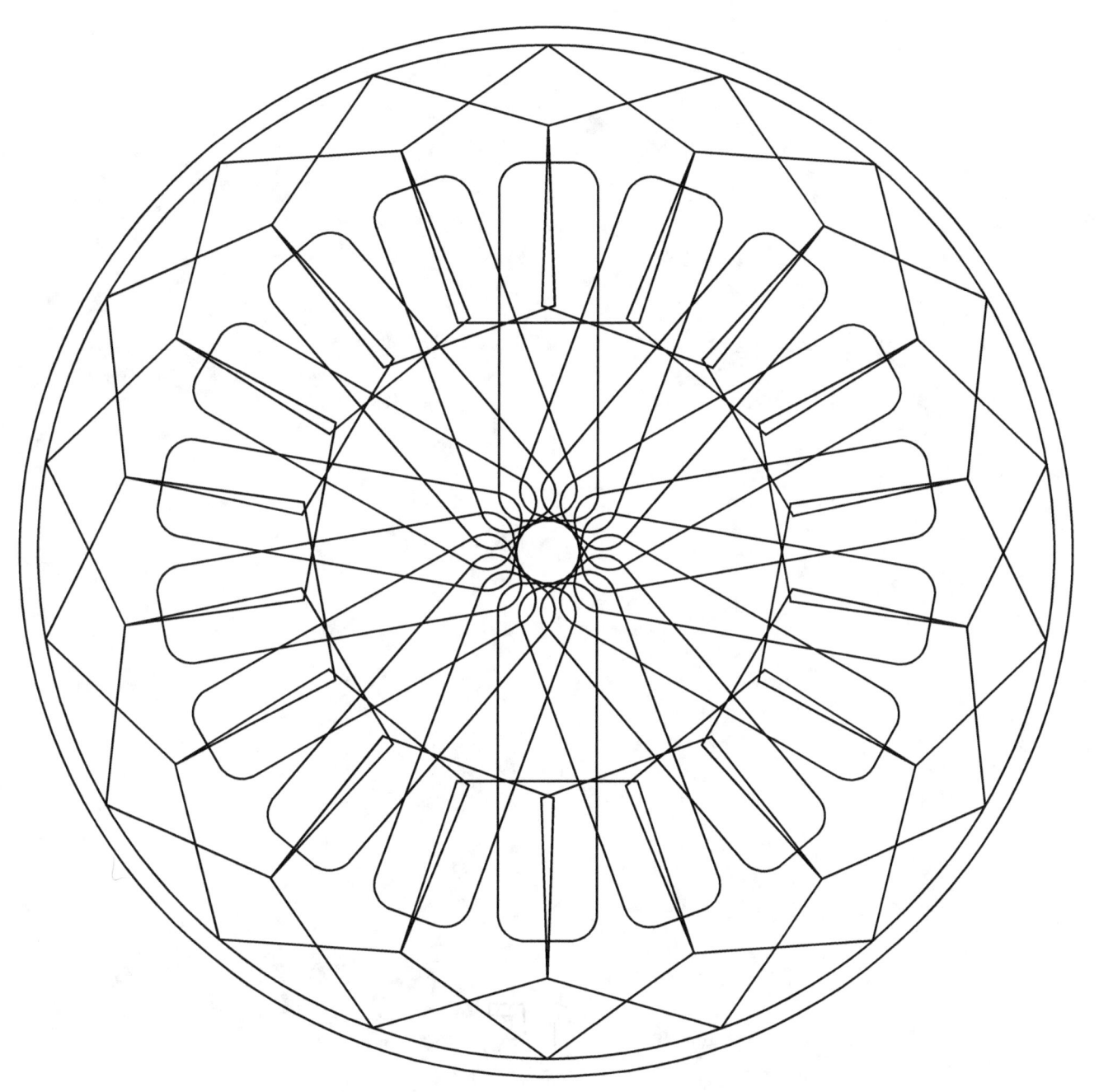

15

When you're done, take a pic and share on Instagram using
#FantasticalColouring

Copyright©2020 Imran Mughal

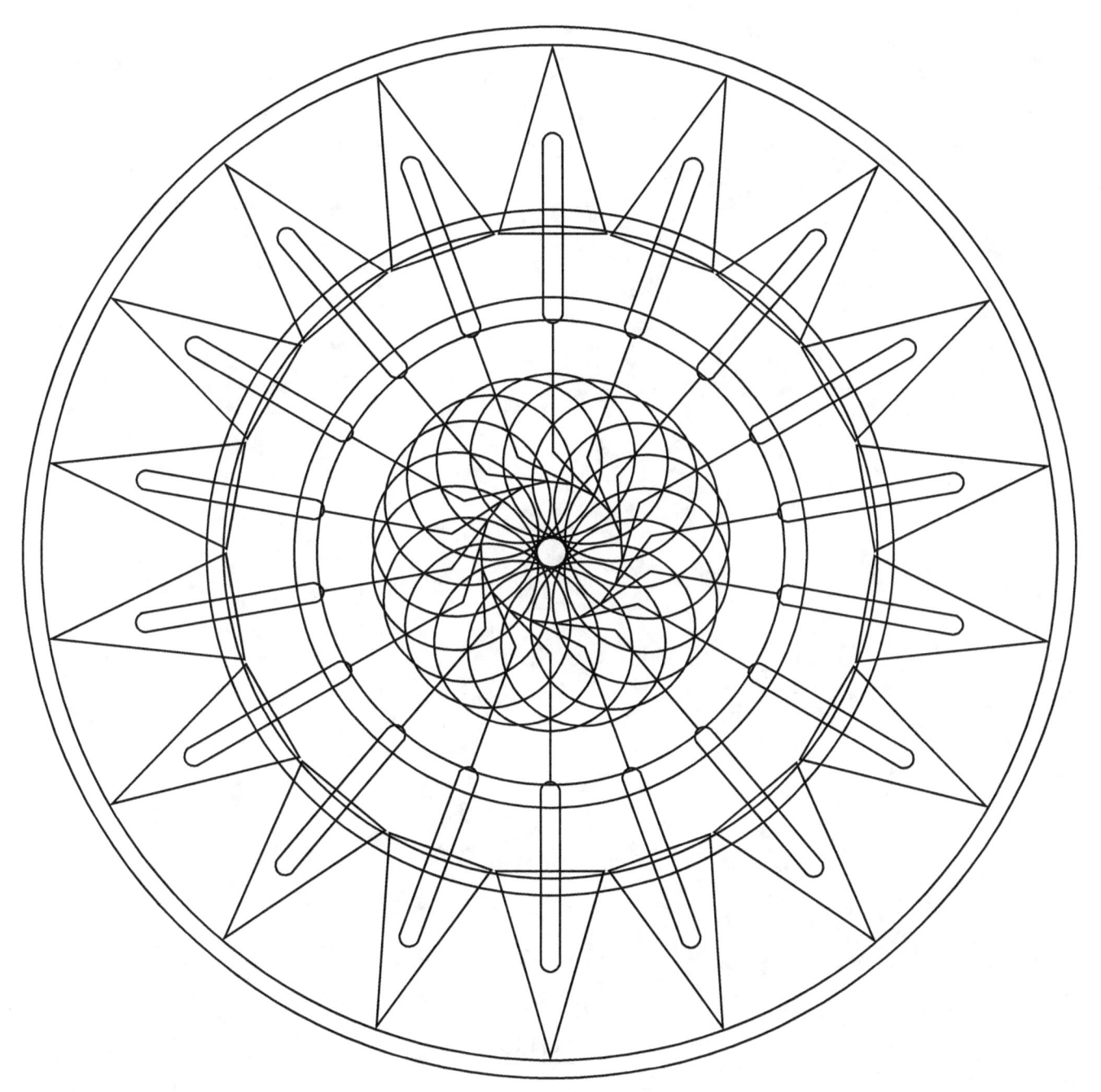

When you're done, take a pic and share on Instagram using
#FantasticalColouring

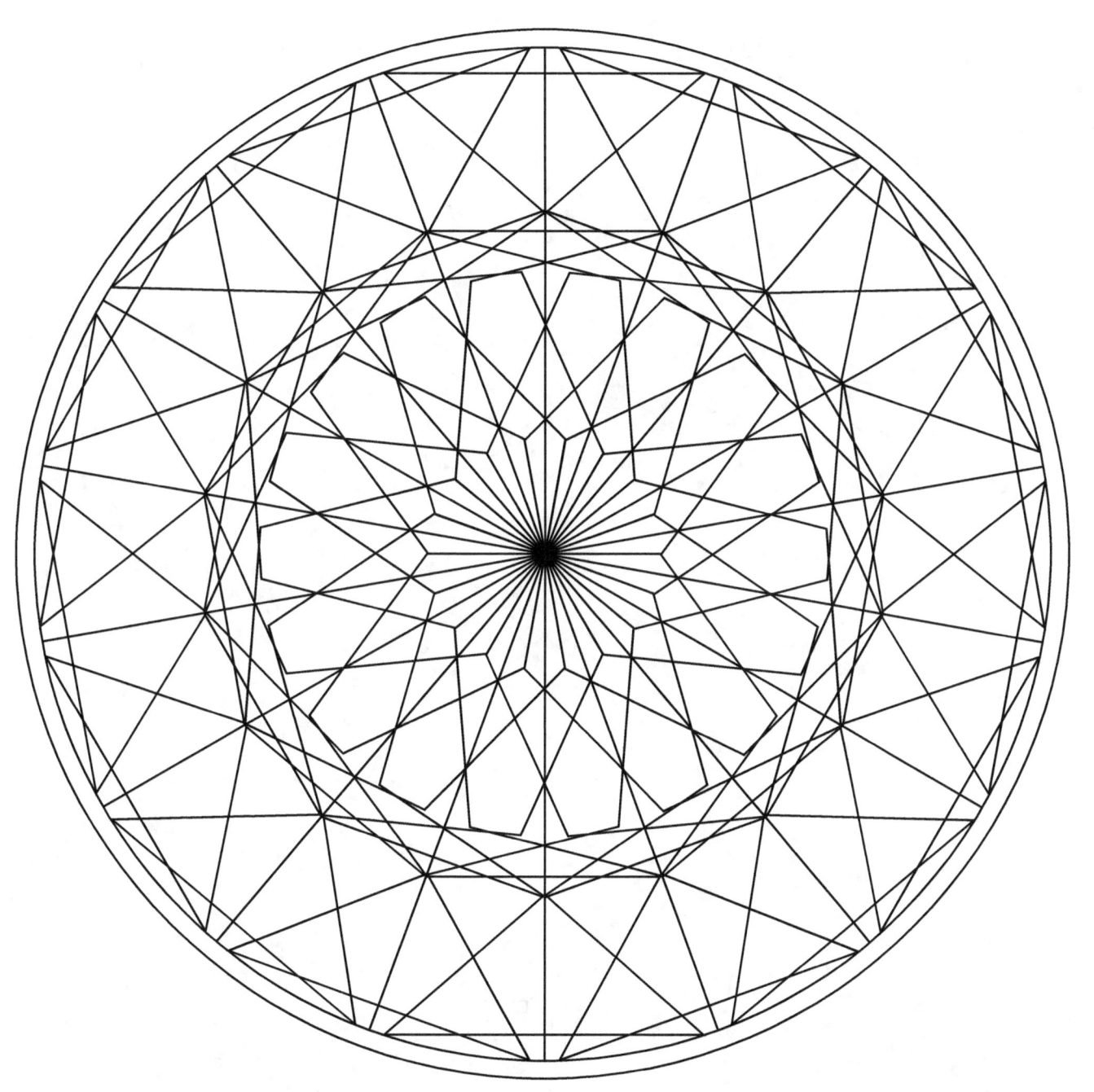

17

When you're done, take a pic and share on Instagram using
#FantasticalColouring

Copyright©2020 Imran Mughal

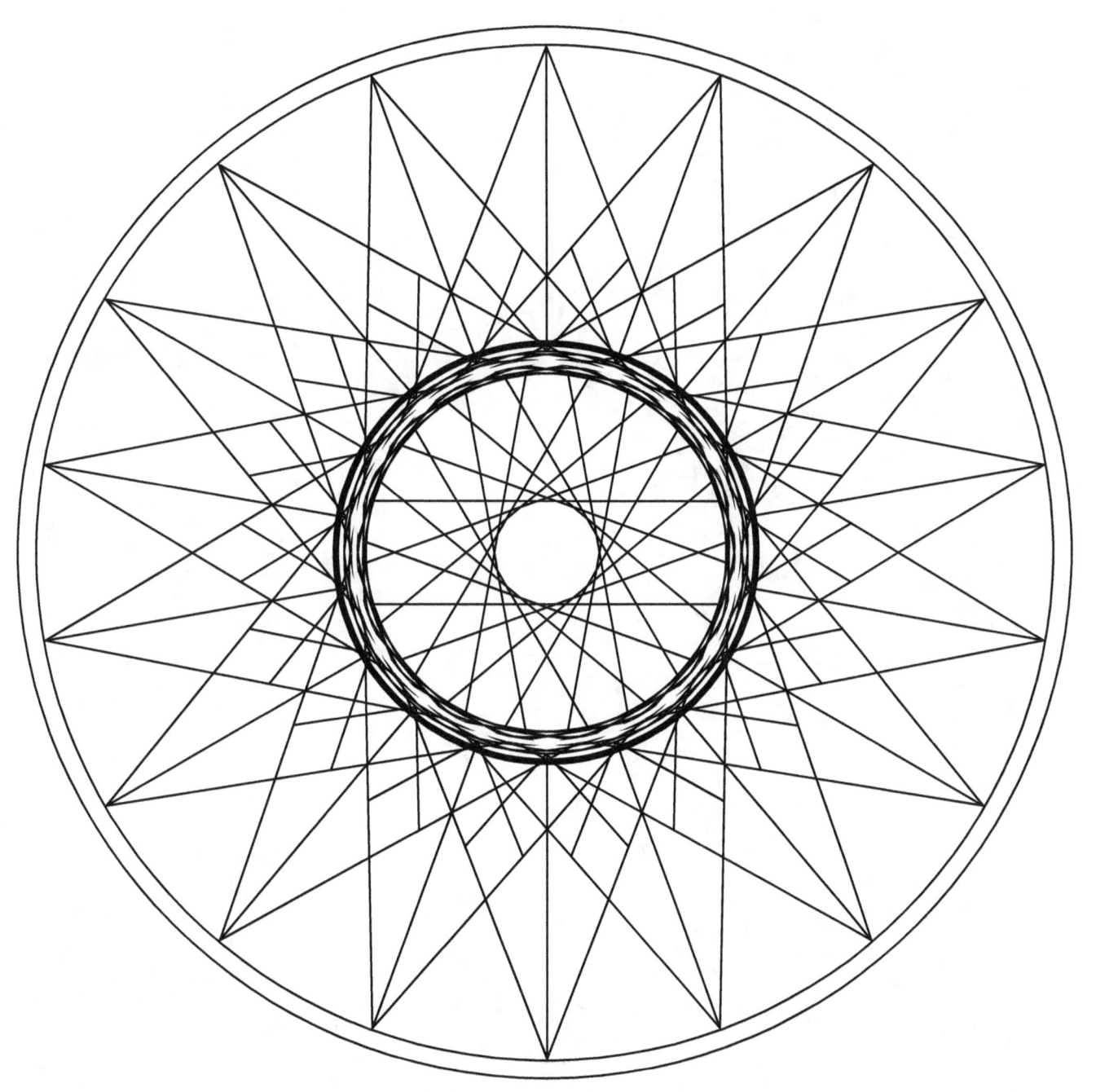

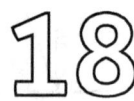

When you're done, take a pic and share on Instagram using
#FantasticalColouring

Copyright©2020 Imran Mughal

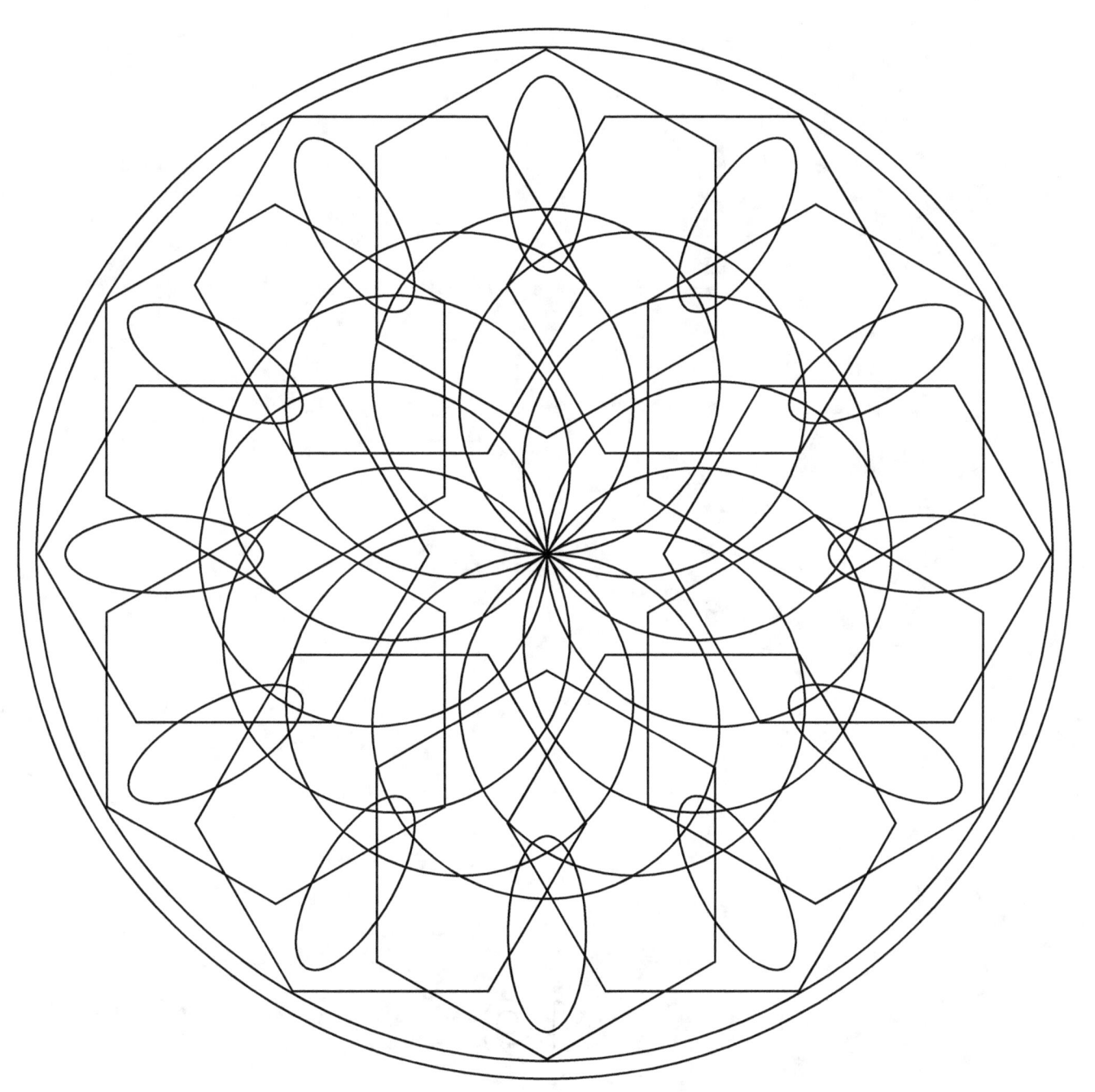

19

When you're done, take a pic and share on Instagram using
#FantasticalColouring

Copyright©2020 Imran Mughal

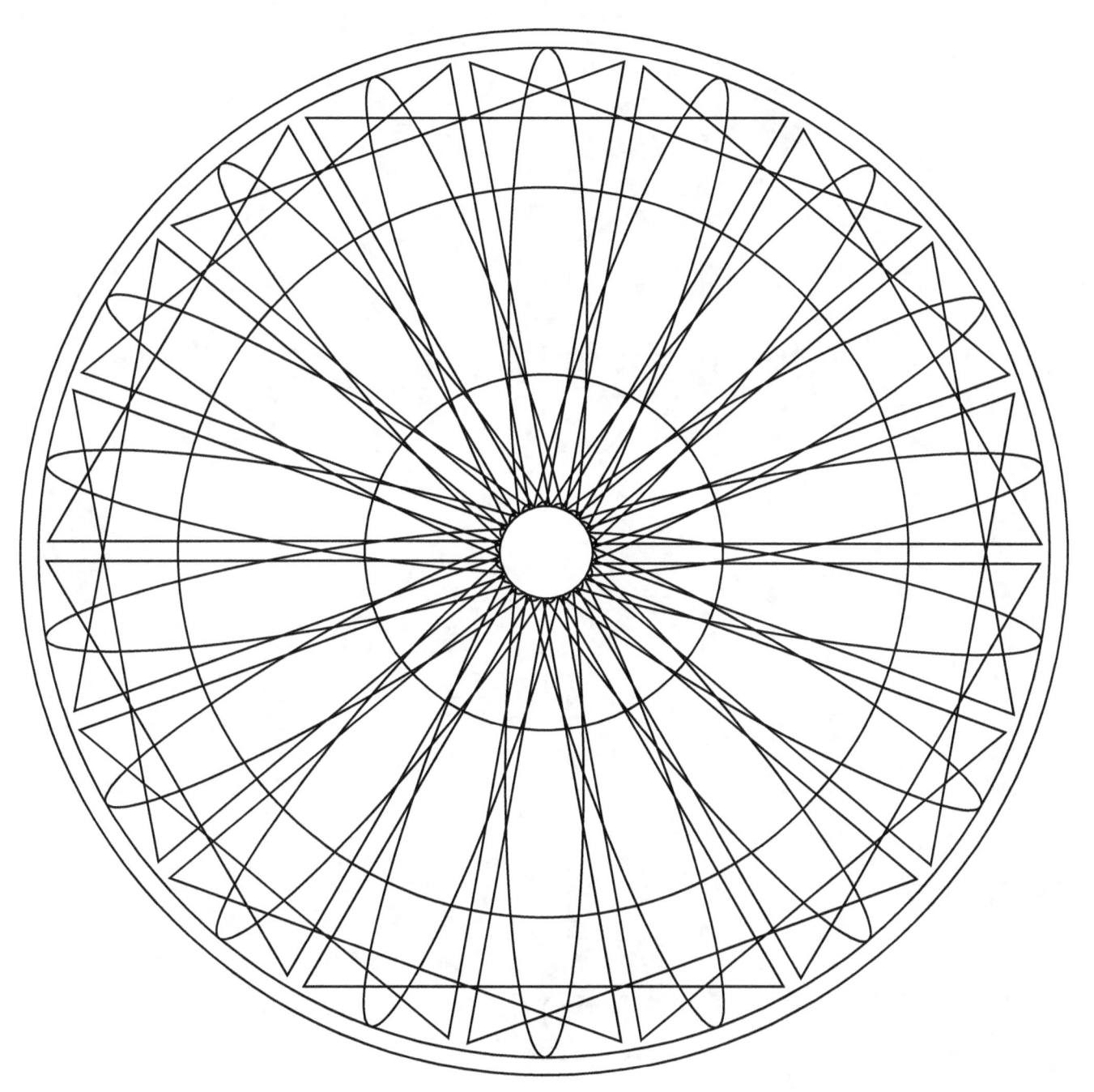

20

When you're done, take a pic and share on Instagram using
#FantasticalColouring

Copyright©2020 Imran Mughal

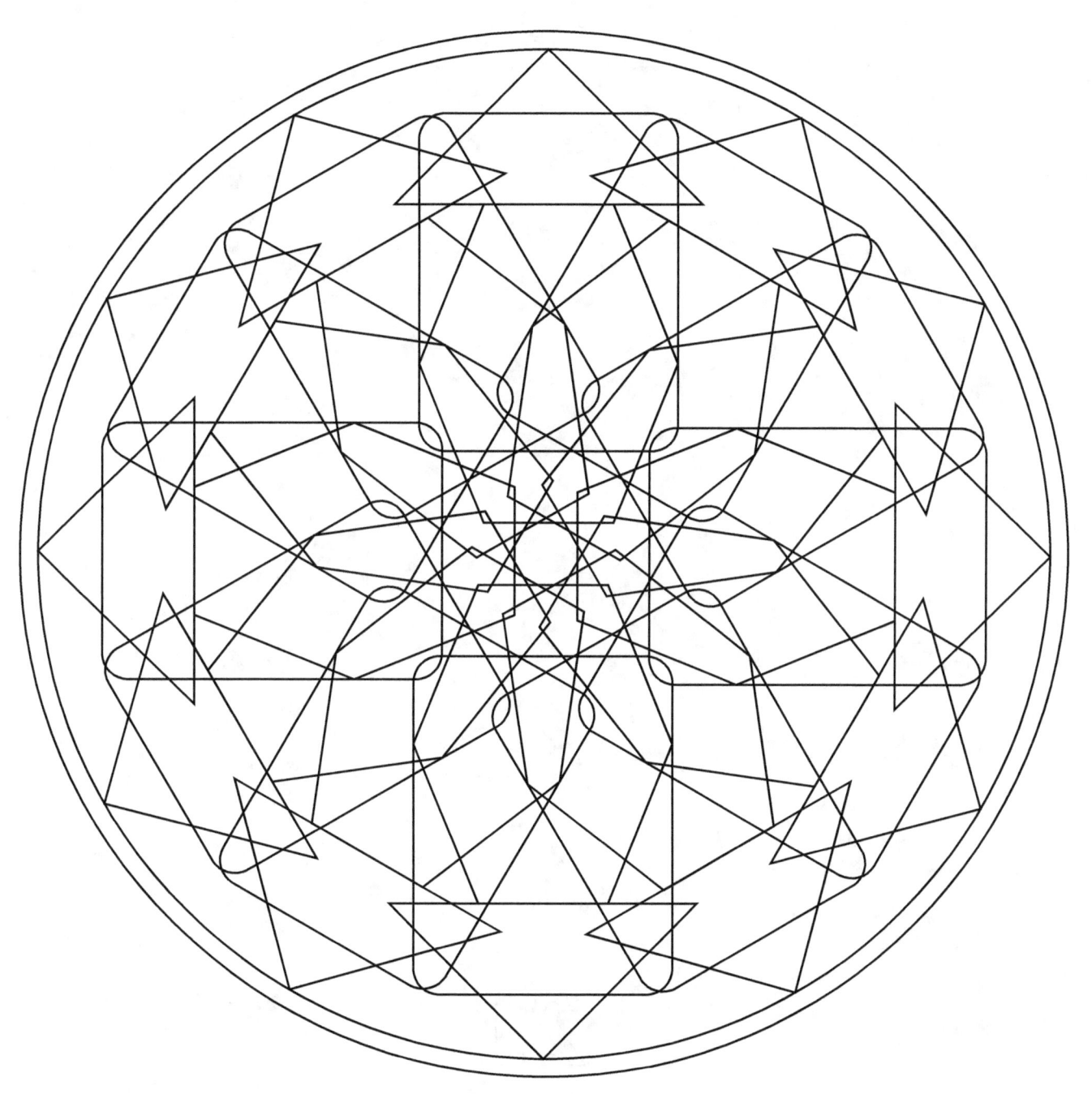

21

When you're done, take a pic and share on Instagram using
#FantasticalColouring

Copyright©2020 Imran Mughal

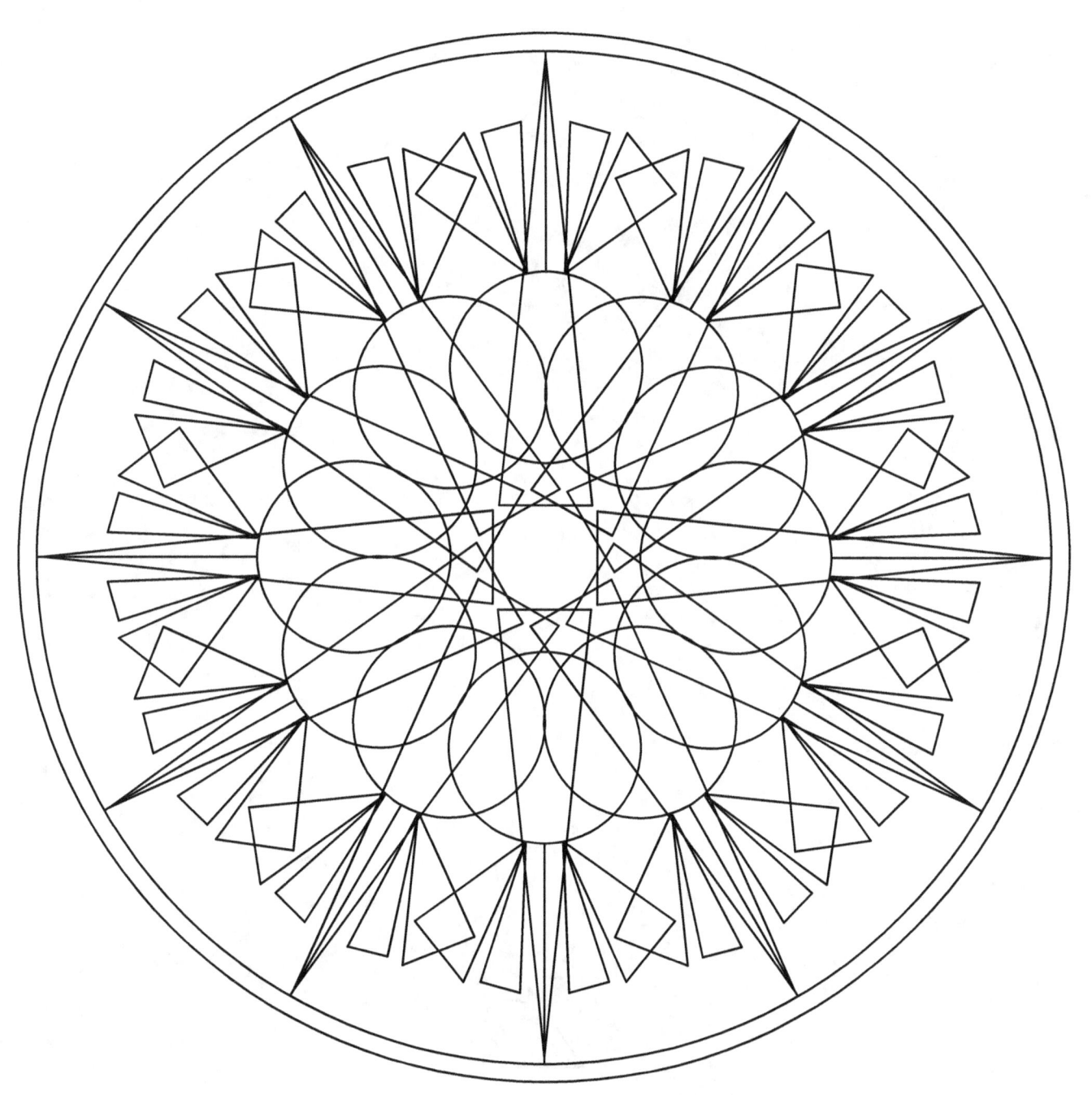

22

When you're done, take a pic and share on Instagram using
#FantasticalColouring

Copyright©2020 Imran Mughal

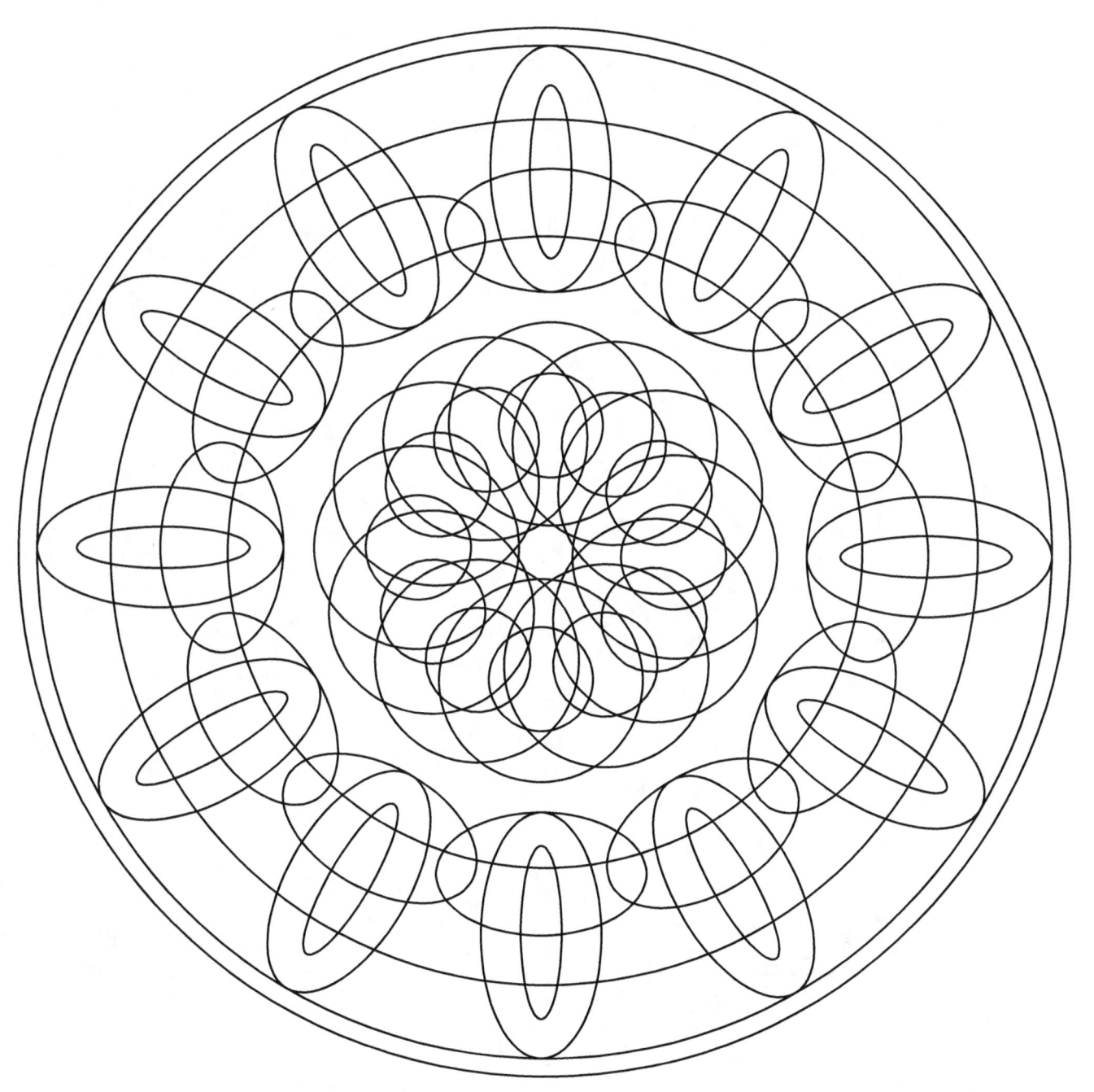

23

When you're done, take a pic and share on Instagram using
#FantasticalColouring

Copyright©2020 Imran Mughal

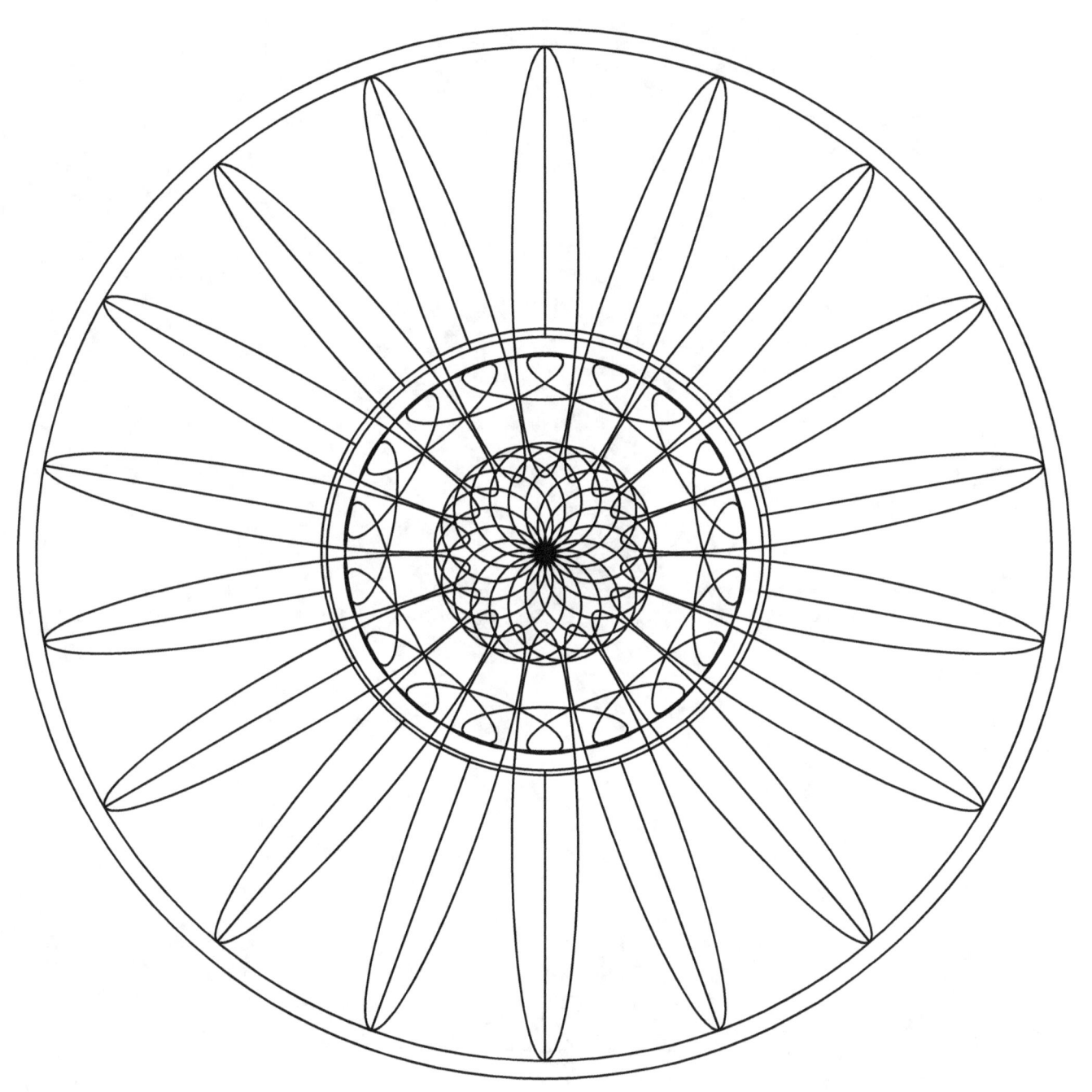

24

When you're done, take a pic and share on Instagram using
#FantasticalColouring

Copyright©2020 Imran Mughal

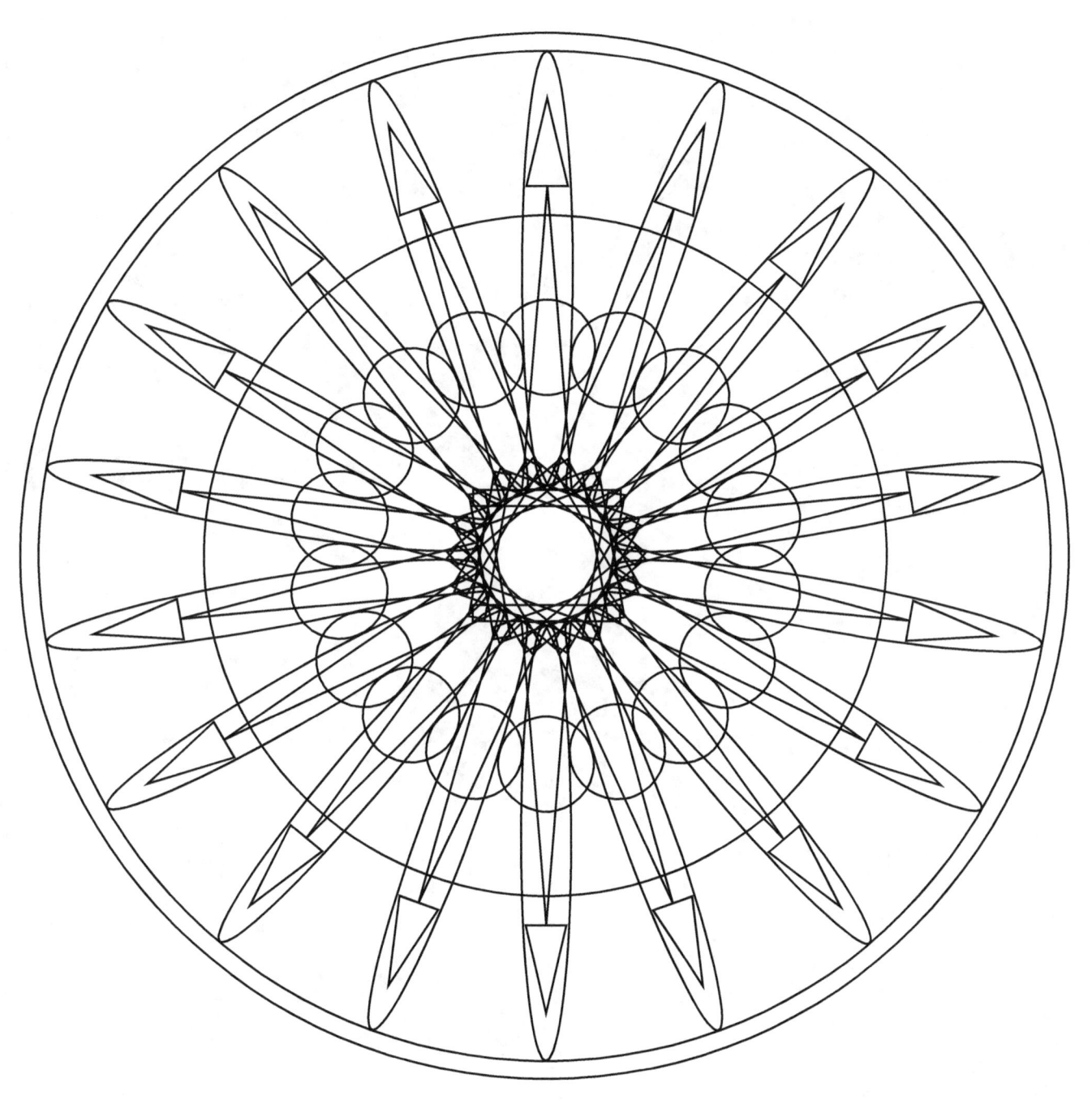

25

When you're done, take a pic and share on Instagram using
#FantasticalColouring

Copyright©2020 Imran Mughal

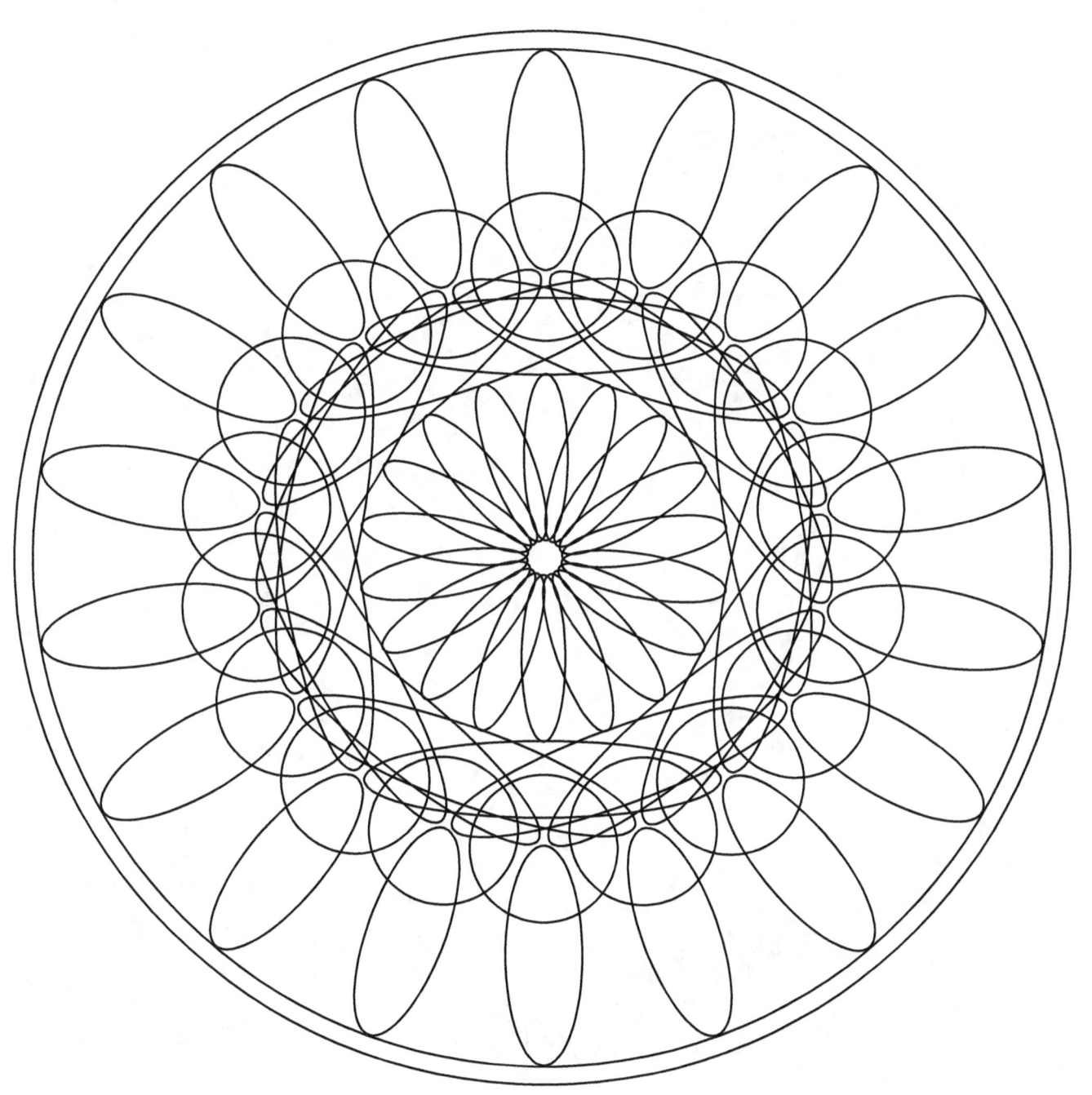

26

When you're done, take a pic and share on Instagram using
#FantasticalColouring

Copyright©2020 Imran Mughal

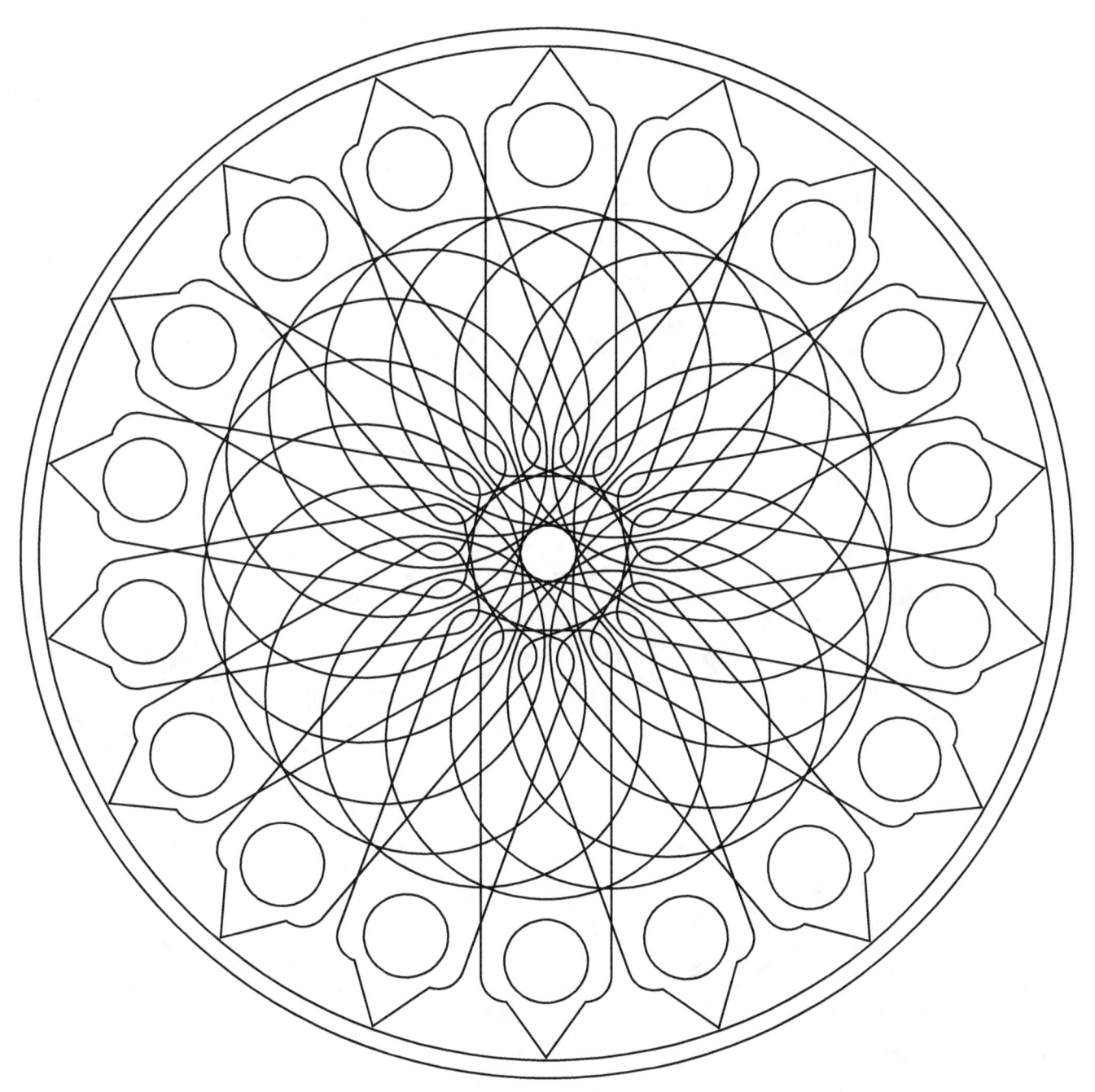

27

When you're done, take a pic and share on Instagram using
#FantasticalColouring

Copyright©2020 Imran Mughal

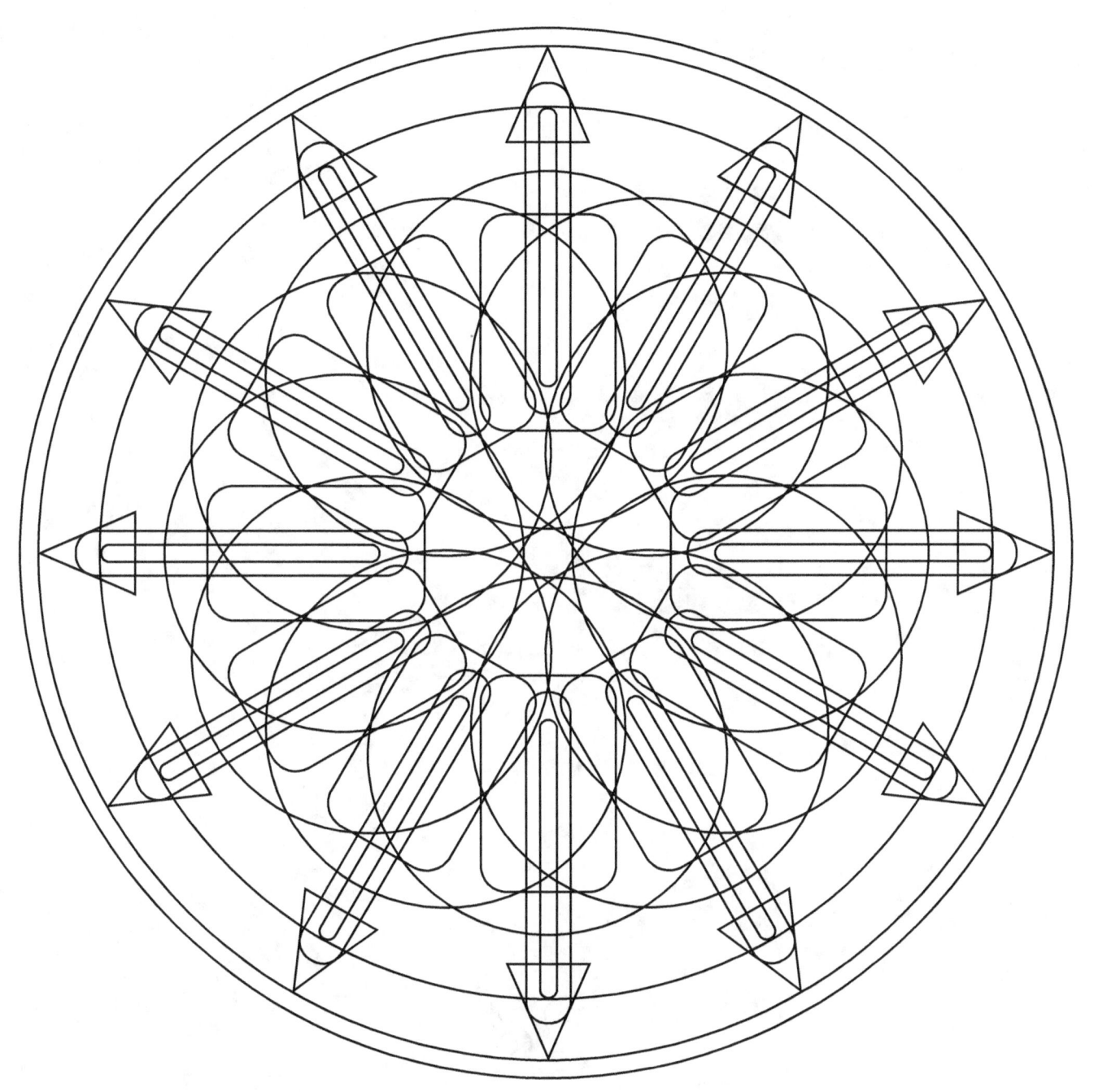

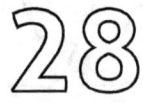

When you're done, take a pic and share on Instagram using
#FantasticalColouring

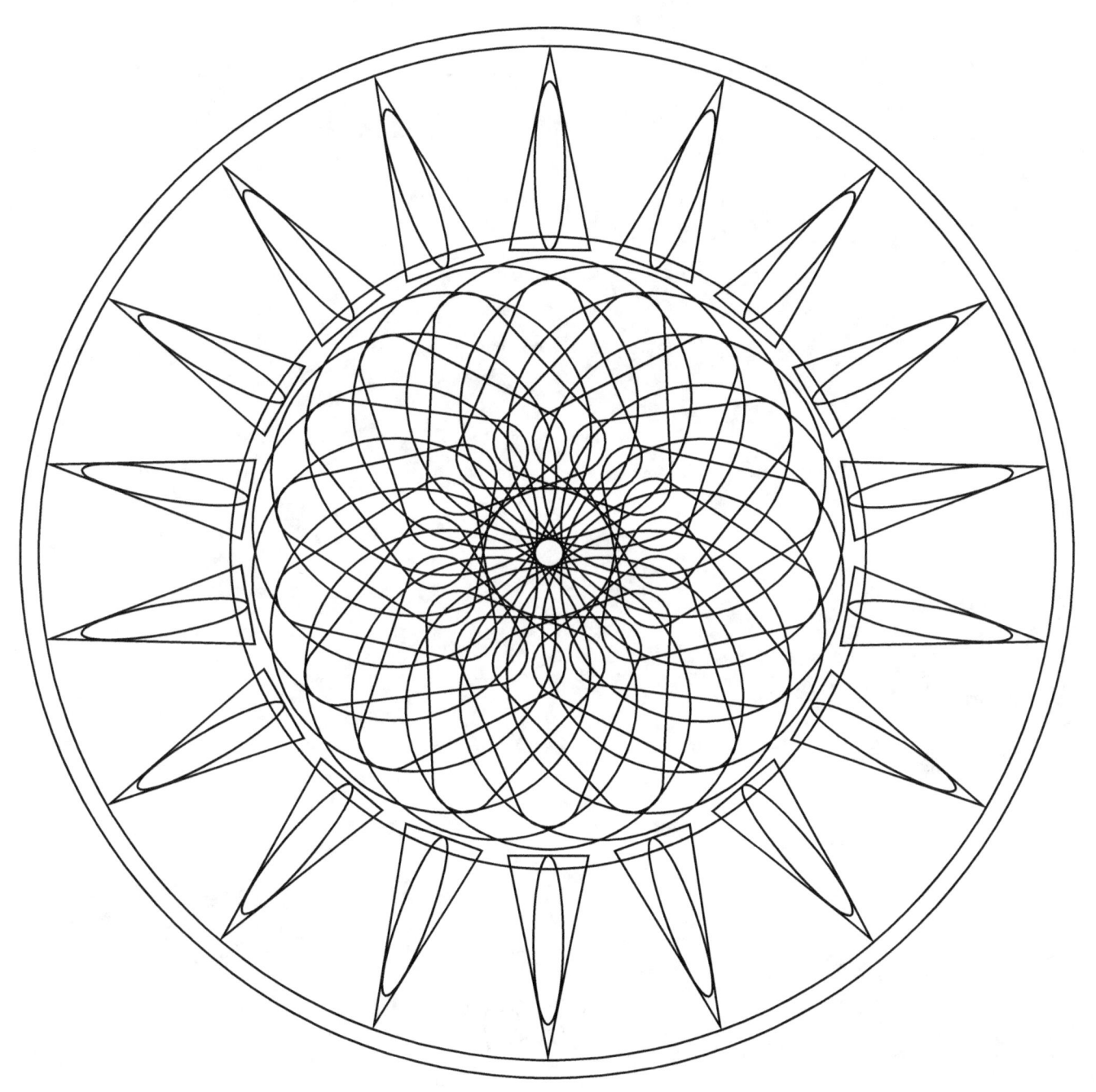

When you're done, take a pic and share on Instagram using
#FantasticalColouring

Copyright©2020 Imran Mughal

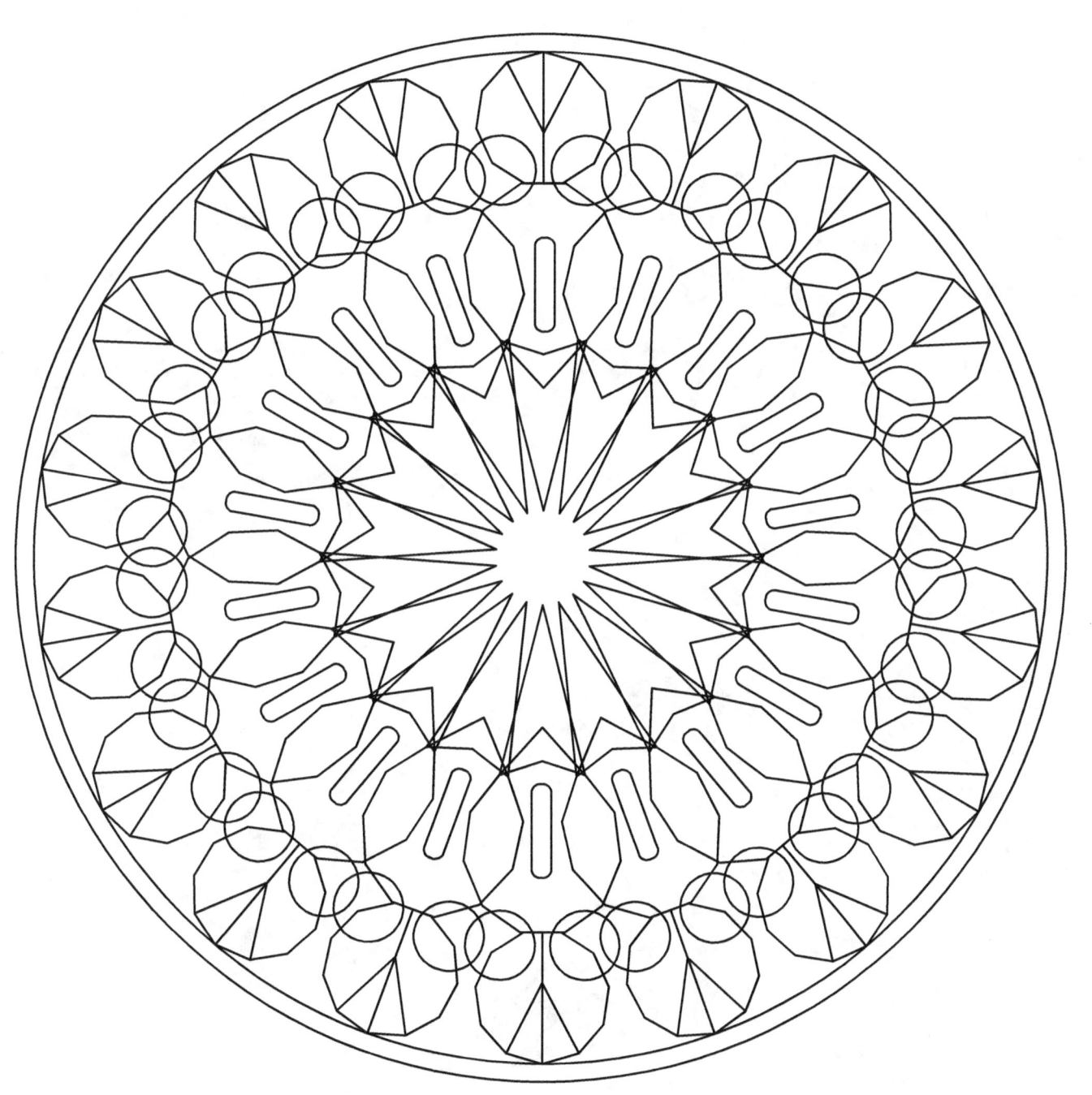

30

When you're done, take a pic and share on Instagram using
#FantasticalColouring

Copyright©2020 Imran Mughal

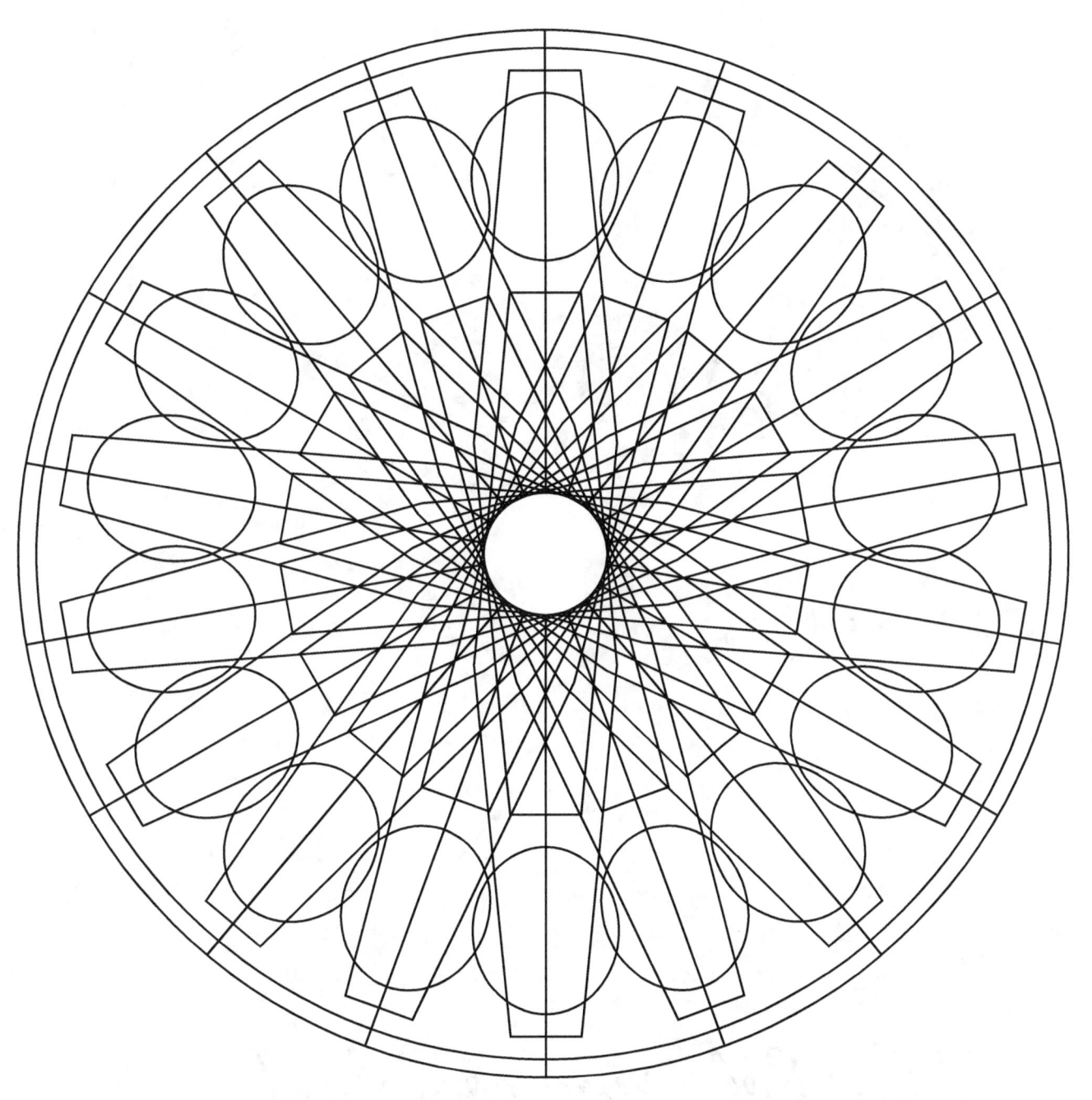

Colouring complete!

...now get ready for volume 2!

KEEP AN EYE OUT FOR **THE LATEST RELEASES** IN THE FANTASTICAL COLOURING BOOK SERIES!

Scan QR code to view all published books in this series and more:

Stay connected for the latest news on book releases and competitions by following this series on:

Instagram **@FantasticalColouring**
#FantasticalColouring

Interested in art, design and illustration?
Then check out my channels on Instagram and YouTube

@SketchingFineArt
#SketchingFineArt

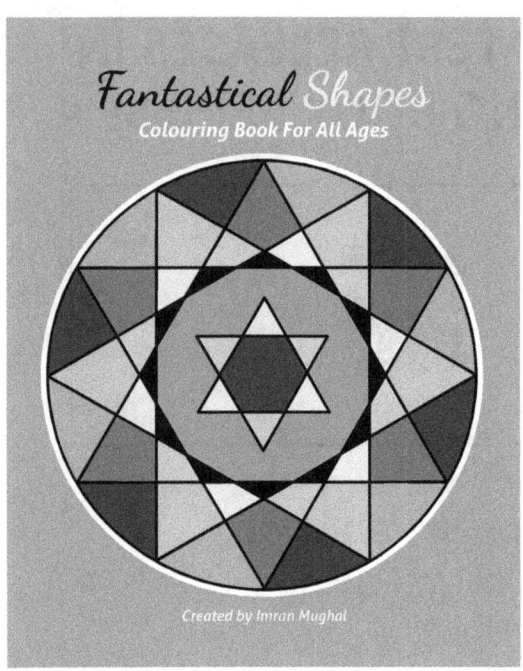

Fantastical Shapes Colouring Book for all ages

20 simple patterns for *colourists of all ages* to enjoy colouring in!

Scan QR code:

Only available on Amazon - get your copy today!

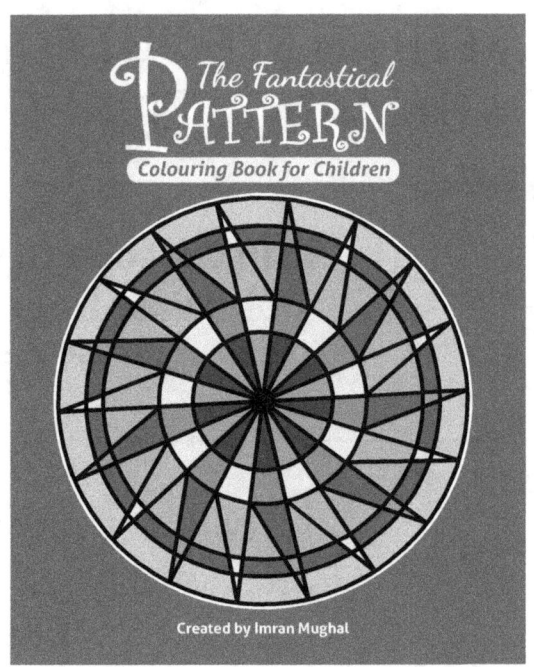

The Fantastical Pattern Colouring Book for Children

20 simple patterns for *the youngest of colourists* to enjoy in a fun, relaxing, colouring in session!

Scan QR code: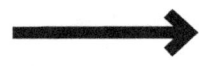

Only available on Amazon - get your copy today!

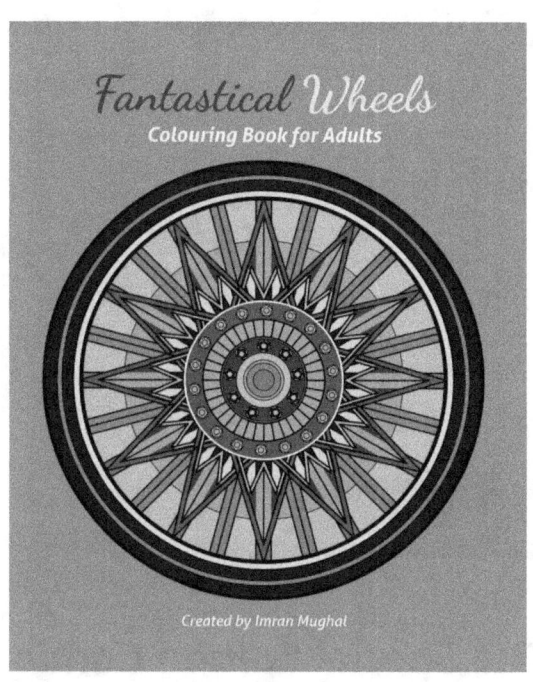

Fantastical Wheels Colouring Book for Adults & Young Car Enthusiasts

20 intricate wheel patterns for *adults and enthusiastic young colourists* to enjoy colouring in!

Scan QR code:

Only available on Amazon - get your copy today!

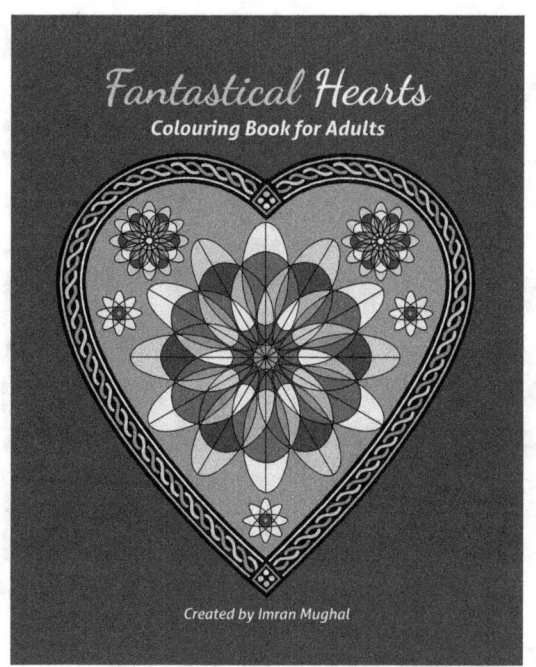

Fantastical Hearts Colouring Book for Adults

20 intricate heart patterns for *adults and enthusiastic young colourists* to enjoy colouring in!

Scan QR code:

Only available on Amazon - get your copy today!

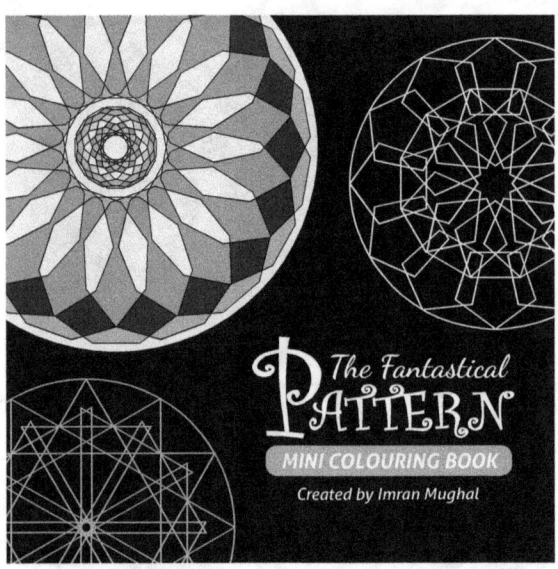

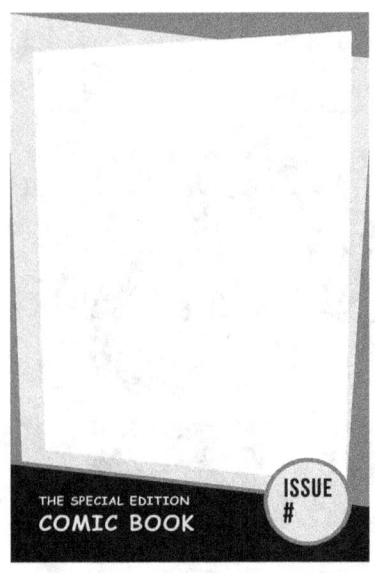

The Fantastical Pattern Mini Colouring Book

11 intricate patterns created with 11 different shapes for *adults and enthusiastic young colourists* to enjoy colouring in!

Scan QR code:

Only limited copies available - Get your copy from Etsy today before they run out!

The Special Edition Comic Book Maker

Create your own complete modern comic book with your own covers for *all comic book enthusiasts*!

Scan QR code:

Only available on Amazon - get your copy today!

Test your mediums here...

www.ingramcontent.com/pod-product-compliance
Lightning Source LLC
Chambersburg PA
CBHW081457220526
45466CB00008B/2683